TALK YOUR WAY TO SUCCESS

Originally published as *Professionally Speaking*

by

Lilyan Wilder

Foreword by John Naisbitt

A Fireside Book
Published by Simon & Schuster, Inc.
NEW YORK

Copyright © 1986 by Lilyan Wilder
All rights reserved
including the right of reproduction
in whole or in part in any form
First Fireside Edition, 1987
Published by Simon & Schuster, Inc.
Simon & Schuster Building
Rockefeller Center
1230 Avenue of the Americas
New York, New York 10020
Originally published by Simon and Schuster as *Professionally Speaking*
FIRESIDE and colophon are registered trademarks of Simon & Schuster, Inc.
Designed by Carla Weise/Levavi & Levavi
Manufactured in the United States of America

10 9 8 7 6 5 4 3 2   Pbk.

Library of Congress Cataloging-in-Publication Data

Wilder, Lilyan.
    Talk your way to success.

    "Originally published as: Professionally speaking."
    "A Fireside book."
    Includes index.
    1. Public speaking. 2. Voice culture. I. Title.
PN4121.W387   1987   808.5′1   87-8641
ISBN 0-671-63956-0 Pbk.

(continued at the back of the book)

To Irving

ACKNOWLEDGMENTS

Of the many experiences I have had in writing this book only one was more surprising than the overall exhilaration and satisfaction. And that is, I have learned what it means to have the support and attention of friends.

Some old friendships deepened and some new friendships were made in the sharing of insights with the people who helped me with this book: Jean Carper, Mark Estren, Harriet Englander, Mary Esch (who did the diagrams for voice and articulation), Gilroye A. Griffin, Peter Herford, Donald Hutter, Linda C. Jones, Noel Katz, Margaret Loft, Laurie Lister, Elizabeth Martin, Lawrence McQuade, Maureen Orth, Ray Price, Catherine Shaw, Sandra Sheppard, John Striker, Grant Tate, Alma Varvaro (whose impeccable fashion sense is a continuing inspiration), and Paul Wilson. I am very grateful.

In the Rodgers and Hammerstein musical *The King and I*, one of the song lyrics underscores my own discovery—that if you become a teacher, you'll be taught by your students. And so, to my students, for all the lessons I have learned from you, my heartfelt thanks.

I wish that I could repeat the names of the generous people, named and unnamed in this book, who gave of their time and experiences in interviews. They have contributed greatly.

And thanks, too, to Dennis Hawver of The Hawver Group, who did the research on, and provided the survey of, middle managers.

Finally, and from the beginning, two very special people gave consistently of their intelligence, talent and soul to the life of this book. Katherine Kormendi and Priscilla Shanks have my enduring appreciation.

CONTENTS

PART TWO: ALL YOU NEED TO KNOW TO GET YOUR MESSAGE ACROSS: THE LILYAN WILDER PROGRAM (STEPS ONE–THREE)

PART THREE: HOW TO SOUND YOUR BEST: THE LILYAN WILDER PROGRAM (Step Four)

FOREWORD

Many say we are becoming a civilization of illiterates. But our concept of literacy is also radically changing. That's what this book is about. It's more than about how to speak successfully; it's a plea for a new literacy of the human voice, with instructions from a skillful teacher about how to achieve a new competence in oral communication so necessary for survival in this revolutionary age of information.

Literacy, according to most dictionaries, is a static term: the ability to read and write. But today's literacy is dynamic and must be measured by an ability to handle the language currency of the day. And the definition of who is literate and who isn't—or who will be—is undergoing shock-wave changes as the old industrial society falls away and the new society founded on the ability to process and transmit information takes over.

It is true there is a crisis in traditional literacy. Some recent national reports condemn the products of our educational system. According to one, 28 million Americans are functionally illiterate—unable to read, write or handle the language. The Carnegie Council of Policy Studies in Higher Education recently reported that "because of deficits in our public school system, about one third of our youth are ill-educated, ill-employed and ill-equipped to make their way in American society." For the first time in history, youngsters graduating from high school are less skilled than their parents. There is a generation gap in traditional literacy.

At the same time, the prospects for a new literacy are exhilarating. Just think, we have invented a whole new literacy in the last decade—the computer word, peculiar to our generation alone. And coupled with that is a revival of our oral tradition, the first in five hundred years, since it was squashed by the invention of the printing press. Virtually everyone recognizes the emergence of the high-technology literacy, the ability to manipulate the language of the computer. As I noted in *Megatrends*, those without such computer literacy will be condemned in the future to wandering around the library of knowledge without a Dewey decimal system, card catalogue or librarian to guide them—denied access to the very information that underlies their society.

On the other hand, almost totally ignored is the emergence of a counterpoint to the new computer literacy that is just as important to making our way in the informational new world: the ability to communicate effectively in the oral language. If one side of the new literacy coin is the computer word, the flip side is the spoken word. That they are coming into prominence together should not be surprising.

High technology—in this case computers—always brings with it a counterbalancing human response, what I call the "high touch" response. The more high-tech, the more high-touch. Without the high-touch reaction, the high technology will be rejected by society.

What could be a more logical "high-touch" counterpart to the cold, steely voice of the computer than the human voice? We find it all around us: oral communication, the most compelling way to reach one another. Surely, the prime examples are radio and television. The endless spoken word. And although many complain that the message is empty, it need not be that way, nor is it likely to continue that way as television matures, becomes more decentralized and video capabilities fall into everybody's hands (as is already happening with the wide distribution of home video equipment). In business and politics, too, decentralization brings confrontation on more personal levels, where human speech carries the message. Conference calls are becoming more common, for example, and major political decisions are increasingly being made at community meetings. In the "global village," as in real villages, people will be thrown closer together, where they will be forced to communicate more effectively. It has even been predicted that our preoccupation with materialistic consumption of goods may give way to a nonmaterialistic consumption of human relationships requiring more intimate interactions.

So it's hardly such a shocking prospect to get back to talking to each other—instead of primarily writing to each other. After all, our oral tradition is of much longer duration than our printed tradition. The printing press, the invention that brought reading and writing literacy to the masses, is only five hundred years old, compared with untold centuries of oral communication.

As the movie *Quest for Fire* made clear, the humanizing of the race came with oral language. The language we grew heir to, for hundreds of thousands of years, was oral—grunts, sounds, words, sentences, whole epic poems passed from generation to generation by great storytellers. The tales of Homer were centuries old before they were "written down." The ancient Egyptians dictated to scribes. In medieval England the definition of literacy was to recite in Latin. Poetry, mostly silent today, was originally conceived for the ear. And when the printing press overthrew the long history of oral communication, the scholars of the day mourned and decried the destruction of literacy. What would happen to human memory, they asked, when ideas could so easily be transferred to paper for everyone to read? It's somewhat the same way the high priests of the written word are rising to protect today's traditional literacy against intrusions by computers and television.

But the new literacy is unstoppable, and those who understand it and grasp it will be the winners of the future. It is a skill necessary for survival and success in the new informational society. And just as the language of the computer must be learned, so must the forgotten language of the spoken word. Few of us do it very well. We are out of practice. And unfortunately, most of us think we cannot learn. We believe that our voices, our speech patterns, our ability to communicate are natural, as immutable as our fingerprints. We mistakenly think that actresses and actors and "great communicators" in business and politics were born with the voices and abilities to get across their messages.

Those of us who have studied with Lilyan Wilder know that is not true. We know that the voice is subject to enormous changes in tone and volume and warmth. We know that our thoughts need not only to be written down but to be thrown out there with force, wit, sensitivity and meaning, so that they can be picked up by other human beings. We also know that these skills are not merely for a select few. The measure of the new literacy is that everyone will need to acquire it.

There are many teachers of computer science but few teachers of human communication and speech. Lilyan Wilder is unquestionably one of the most notable. She has long privately taught some of the best communicators in the country. By putting her years of experience, sensitivity, secrets and advice into a book, she is providing everyone with access to the new literacy of the future, where the human voice is fully as important as the computer voice.

JOHN NAISBITT,
author of *Megatrends*
July 1985

INTRODUCTION

My whole method consists of enabling students to have an experience. I try to plan for them things to do, things to think about, contacts to make. When they have had that experience well and deeply, it is possible to point out what it is and why it has brought these results.

The real laws of art, the basic laws, are few.

—Kimon Nicolaides
The Natural Way to Draw, 1941

Thursday, September 27, 1984. The phone rings. "This is Vice President Bush's office," said the voice at the other end of the line. "The vice president is inviting you to a rehearsal of his debate with Geraldine Ferraro this Monday." I had nine appointments scheduled for Monday. I asked if the rehearsal could be videotaped so that I could critique it from New York. The woman at the other end said she would call back. Twenty minutes later the phone rang again. "There will not be a videotape made. The vice president would like you to attend the rehearsal. You will have fifteen minutes with him afterward." I said I would be there.

I had been working with George Bush since late 1978 when he decided to throw his hat in the ring for the presidency in 1980. He had come to my office at the insistence of a close associate who knew how important it was to sharpen communication skills before a political campaign began. George, however, was not sold on the idea of working with a communications consultant. He was resistant to the idea of being "made over." He wanted to win, but he wanted to win because of who he really was and what he had accomplished; because of his intelligence and strength of character; and the authority he'd acquired through a lifetime of private achievement and public service as president of his own oil company, congressman, ambassador to the United Nations, ambassador to China, and director of the CIA. Besides, the demands on his time were fierce; his skills as a public speaker seemed good enough to him already.

In fact, back in 1978 George Bush was an adequate speaker. He came across as a man of intelligence and authority. He had strong convictions about what he was saying, as well as a winning, natural warmth. He felt comfortable before large crowds.

All this became clear to me during our first visit, as he practiced the speech he was to give to the Republican Booster Club in New York City. And the first thing I did when he had finished was to point out his intrinsic strengths as a communicator. I reassured him that I didn't want to make him over. I wasn't in the market for grafting cosmetic images onto real people. What life and experience had already given him were the most precious resources he had as a communicator. All I wanted to do was to teach him to use these assets more fully, to help him bring his own unique self more to the fore, so that the connection he made to an audience was strong, positive and personal. At present he wasn't doing himself justice.

As we went over the practice videotape I'd made, I pointed out that his ideas could have been structured to come through more clearly. Excess verbiage and abrupt, unnecessary gestures were getting in the way of his message. A slight New England twang interfered with the warmth and vitality behind his words.

I could see George's mind start to click. He began to catch a glimpse of the kind of speaker he could become, of how much more effective *and true* the videotape speech could have been with the changes I was suggesting. This kind of work was worth a serious investment of his time. He was convinced.

As our sessions progressed we tackled his verbal skills. I tape recorded some of George's speeches and transcribed them verbatim. He was amazed to note the sea of words on each page and began to fix the problem almost immediately. I then showed him how to mark a text so that key words and thoughts would stand out for him as well as the listener. We also worked at refining his body language. He had a tendency to point his finger and hit the lectern for emphasis. Videotaping convinced him of how distracting these gestures were, and he began to substitute smoother movements.

As we continued to work on particular skills, not only did the personal and professional strengths of which George was already aware come through more and more clearly, personal qualities ("colors") he'd either been unaware of or had dismissed as unstatesmanlike—his low-key humor and boyish charm, for example—began to emerge. And the more sure he became of himself as a communicator, the freer and more spontaneous he became as well.

George Bush, who had been so skeptical, turned into a committed, enthusiastic student of oral communication. Whenever I sent him a written critique of a particular speech or TV appearance, he responded with a handwritten memo. Now, six years of hard work were to culminate in what would perhaps be the most critical speaking engagement of his career. He was to debate Geraldine Ferraro, the vice presidential candidate on the Democratic ticket, on national television.

This debate was of crucial importance to both Bush himself and to the presidential campaign. President Reagan had not done well in his recent debate with Walter Mondale—it was said, among other things, that Reagan's age had been noticeable—and it fell to George Bush to rally support and solidify the Republican ticket. Adding to the pressure was the growing popularity of Geraldine Ferraro. As the first woman nominated for vice president on a major party ticket, she was drawing large crowds everywhere. Hungry for campaign dramatics, the news media had built this debate into a major confrontation.

When I arrived at the Old Executive Office Building next door to the White House for the first rehearsal, I was directed to a small auditorium.

His closest advisors waited for the vice president's arrival. When at last he walked in, it was clear that he was exhausted. I was shocked to see how thin and gaunt he had become. Campaigning in two or three states a day was obviously taking its toll. He was clearly overworked and had not yet been able to take the time to prepare for this event. Some of his answers to the tough, hostile questions fired off by four people acting as reporters lacked impact. His interactions with Mrs. Ferraro's stand-in were sometimes defensive and at other times aggressive.

After the rehearsal, I met with Bush in his office and he asked for my comments.

"Number one," I said, "don't think of Ferraro as an opponent. In a debate you've got to be gracious and noncombative because hostility works against you." I had been making notes for him on 3×5 cards, and I handed one to him on which I'd written an oriental proverb: "If you wish your merit to be known, acknowledge that of other people." "What is it about Ferraro that you admire?" I asked. He thought a moment and said: "I really admire the closeness that she has with her family." "Good," I said. "Let that positive feeling take root in you, and on the day of the debate your warmth toward her will come through, and your delivery is bound to be more confident and affable.

"Number two: even though you're preparing for a debate, which by its nature requires that you be spontaneous, you should prepare as you would for a speech. Your responsibility is the same for both occasions. You must get your facts crystal clear in your mind. Then put them in your own words and rehearse that language out loud. Find the time, somewhere between Arkansas and North Carolina, to prepare.

"Number three: be ready to bridge to the point you want to make after answering a question. That way you can control the content of the material to some degree.

"Number four: the facts that you prepare, the answers to questions you think you'll be asked, and the body of information you want to get across form the basis of the 'minispeech'—the technique that we've worked on all these years. Etch that format in your mind.

"Number five: you have the opportunity to work on your conclusion. You will be given [three] minutes air time. Know your closing remarks by heart, and truly believe what you're saying. Prepare and practice."

That first rehearsal proved to be very valuable. It focused the vice president's attention on the issues he wanted to concentrate on. He had the technical aspects of the debate under control, so that during the event itself he'd be free to focus on content.

On October 11, 1984, millions of radios and TV sets were tuned into the Bush-Ferraro debate. That night, George Bush gave himself to the fight. He really wanted to win, and that competitive spirit motivated him to harness all his technical skills and use himself in a real way. As he told me afterward, "As soon as I realized that Mrs. Ferraro wasn't twenty feet tall, I was okay."

Bush kept up the momentum and made sure that he communicated his firsthand experience of Central America and the Soviet Union, and his knowledgeability in the area of terrorism. He fielded tough questions on abortion and nuclear war, and at one point he had the self-confidence to take issue with a reporter who asked: "Was it right for your administration to pursue policies which required those at the bottom of the economic ladder to wait for prosperity to trickle down from those who are much better off?"

"It's not trickling down," Bush asserted, "and I'm not suggesting there's no poverty. I am suggesting the way to work out of poverty is through real opportunity." He went on to discuss the various programs where spending was up and supported his assertions with facts and statistics. Throughout the debate, his voice varied in volume and nuance depending on the content of his words. Bush's energy and ardor were in marked contrast to Geraldine Ferraro, who displayed an uncharacteristic reserve on this occasion.

Of course, there were moments when his performance was not perfect. Occasionally there escaped a spontaneous phrase uncensored by his better judgment. An attempt at humor backfired, and at one point he corrected his own misstated statistic. But these were minor slips that actually served to humanize him. They didn't diminish his competence and commitment.

The vice president spoke with fervor from his heart. This was what moved people: that he was real, and that he cared. He cared about what he was saying, to whom he was saying it and the larger picture, the vision the administration had in mind for America.

A USA Today poll of 586 debate watchers gave Bush a 19 percent point margin, 48 percent to 29 percent over Ferraro.

"I really felt it was George Bush who was seemingly more forceful, more committed, more enthusiastic," said James Ungar, director of the National Forensics Institute, Washington. "I think George Bush really needed to win one for the Gipper, and he did that tonight." "Whatever Reagan lost, Bush got back!" agreed a South Florida Democrat.

Six years ago the vice president had come to me with the same intelligence, insight, and strength of character that had so impressed the nation during the debate. Now, however, he had the confidence to tap deep into the real feelings within himself and share them with an audience of thousands. And, as I have learned from teaching an entire spectrum of students, from politicians to broadcasters to major executives, this and only this will make an otherwise adequate communicator truly outstanding.

For communication is an exchange of life, a dynamic encounter between human beings. If I truly communicate with you, I must move you, stimulate you, arouse your interest, draw you in toward me. I must share myself. Words alone will not achieve it.

Whether I am pleading with you to do something about an urgent situation, describing a technical innovation, or cataloging goals and plans for the future, I must first believe in what I am saying, believe that it matters and speak from my own sense of urgency about the situation or excitement about the innovation. Secondly, I must make a personal connection to you, as one human being to another, whether you're an audience of one or one thousand.

During the 1968 presidential campaign, Robert F. Kennedy paid a visit to a day nursery outside Indianapolis. "Most of the children were from broken homes. 'Two little girls,' wrote David Murray in the *Chicago Sun-Times*, 'came up and put their heads against his waist, and he put his hands on their heads. And suddenly it was hard to watch, because he had become in that moment the father they did not know.... You can build an image with a lot of sharpsters around you with their computers and their press releases. But lonely little children don't come up and put their heads on your lap unless you mean it.'"

At its best, communication can be a totally involving experience for both speaker and listener—emotionally, intellectually and physically—provided the speaker reaches out with everything he has within him: his own physical vitality, his desire to be seen as he truly is and his deepest feelings about what he is saying, what it means to *him*. He gives information and inspiration to his listeners, who respond and stimulate him in return. This sense of true communication is what separates my method from any others that I know. It is the core of my process, both as I teach it one-on-one and as I've laid it out in the chapters to follow. It's what I've come to call "being real." Here is a brief summary of the Lilyan Wilder Four-Step Program.

> *First*, you organize your thoughts and develop your own style of expressing them.
> *Second*, you design your road map, a visual guide to help you emphasize key words and thoughts.
> *Third*, you learn how to practice out loud to prepare for the delivery of your message.
> *Fourth*, you develop your personal sound to express yourself in a voice that truly reflects you. It is your first and lasting impression.

To put these four steps into practice, you learn how to handle the important and difficult communication problems in your nine-to-five day, whether it is selling your ideas to senior management, conducting a staff meeting or dealing with an intimidating boss. You find out how the media works and how to make it work for you.

Finally, you acquire five handy pocket guides. They prepare you for any speaking situation you might face in the next thirty minutes, six hours, six days or six weeks. You also get a four-step guide for media preparation.

This method grows out of a lifetime devoted to communication. It started in the 1940s when Alvina Krause, then the head of the Drama Department at Northwestern University, took me on as her personal assistant when I was still an undergraduate. I assisted in the running of her speech labs and later, after earning an M.A., I began my teaching career at Northwestern with her help. Soon I moved on to Chicago's Teachers College and then to New York City, where I continued my work as an instructor in Voice, Articulation and Public Speaking at Brooklyn and Hunter colleges. I also worked for a year at the New York Hospital for Speech Disorders, where I deepened my understanding of remedial therapeutic techniques.

In 1956 I began my own speech practice. My clients included children with speech defects, executives who wished to sharpen their speaking skills, and actors and actresses. I also designed communications programs for major corporations around the country, including IBM and RCA in California.

During this period, roughly from 1956 to 1969, I also studied singing with Emmy Joseph and worked as an actress in Broadway and off-Broadway plays and on television. The work I did in theater, and especially my studies with Lee Strasberg, fed and enriched my teaching techniques. Strasberg taught me how to delve into my psyche and use my real self as a performer. It is this philosophy that forms the foundation of my program.

In 1969 my work took a new turn. I was teaching Voice and Articulation at the Strasberg Theater Institute when a call came from ABC asking if anyone was interested in coaching an ex-athlete who had been hired as a sportscaster at WFIL-TV (now WPVI-TV) in Philadelphia. Working with Bill White, the former St. Louis Cardinal baseball player, was my entree into a new career as a talent coach to broadcasters. I went on to work with WFIL's chief anchor Larry Kane, and then with the station's affiliates in New Haven, Connecticut, and Buffalo, New York. Soon I was consultant to stations in New York, Boston, Washington, Minneapolis, Denver, Dallas, Los Angeles, San Francisco and other cities across the country.

Currently I work with the three major networks and their stations and affiliates, designing programs tailored to individual needs. In addition, I have private clients, among them talk show hosts, media personalities, authors and politicians. I also work with numerous Fortune 500 corporations, coaching high-profile executives and designing group-training programs for managers and salespeople.

Occasionally, I have returned to academia. In 1972 and '73 I taught on-air delivery techniques to minority students at the Columbia School of Journalism under the auspices of the Michelle Clark Foundation Program.

My book contains information and exercises that are widely applicable, yet I intend it primarily for people in the business world. The broadcasters and politicians who seek my services know that their visibility makes it imperative that they communicate well. The executives who come to my office generally want to prepare themselves for an isolated event—an important speech or an appearance on television. Some want fast results, a quick fix. Others know that to make sense out of the new information age takes effort and commitment to communication skills.

It seems important to return again to the example of George Bush. At first he resisted the idea of a time-consuming program of self-improvement, reasoning that his speaking skills were perfectly adequate. Learning to communicate better gave him the ease and self-confidence to reach into himself and share his feelings with the people listening to him. To persuade and convince, you must reach inside yourself, and that takes more than learning some tricks. That takes real commitment. George Bush took an unsparing look at how he communicated, and he decided to work for change.

With the help of this book, you too can embark on that same rewarding journey. You may not be headed for high political office, but there is no telling how far you can go or how much you can contribute to your organization, your profession and your community, when, like George Bush, you make communicating with excellence a priority in your life.

PART ONE

WHAT IT TAKES TO BE A SUCCESSFUL COMMUNICATOR

Chapter One

THREE
OF
THE BEST

As a kid I went to a concert by Paderewski. . . . I had seats in about the third row. There were two girls sitting next to me with the score. When Paderewski came out, everybody just stood. No clapping, nothing, everyone just stood. He turned a pale, ashen color. . . . Then there was the sound of thousands of people sitting down. And he was obviously very moved; you could see it. He was going to play a Mendelssohn sonata. Well, these girls had their score open, and he saw them. He looked over and said, sort of sotto voce: "You will not find it there, my dears." Boy, they closed that score. And then he proceeded to play.

—Ansel Adams
"The Last interview"
ARTNews, Summer 1984

"The surfer does want to ride the wave to the beach, yet he waits in the ocean for the biggest wave to come along that he thinks he can handle. If he just wanted to be beautiful, he could do that on a medium-sized wave. Why does the surfer wait for the big wave? . . . because he values the challenge it presents. . . . The more challenging the obstacle he faces, the greater the opportunity for the surfer to discover and extend his true potential . . . Note that the surfer in this example is not out to prove himself . . . but is simply involved in the exploration of his latent capacities."

You can experience the same heightened awareness as that of the surfer described by W. Timothy Gallwey in *The Inner Game of Tennis* when you communicate successfully. The difference between *adequate* communication and the *art* of communication is the difference between riding the medium-sized wave and taking on the big wave.

How can I get you to imagine what communication is like when it's an exhilarating experience? The best way I know is to show you three superb communicators in action: Lee Iacocca, Millicent Fenwick and Ted Koppel. I chose them because they are individuals whose enormous success in business, public life and the media literally cannot be separated from the masterful use of the spoken word. And their examples are widely applicable. Each of these great communicators faces the kind of challenges that you as a professional person face in everyday life.

CHALLENGE #1: WINNING THE BATTLE

Imagine this: You've been put in charge of a major account; handed one of your company's most important departments to reorganize; or entrusted with the campaign of the season to handle as you will. Take your pick. But choose something that could make or break your career.

Now imagine this: Things have gone terribly wrong. Yet you believe the situation is salvageable. You know that given one more chance you could turn it around 180 degrees, bring enormous profit to your company, and save your own neck. But no one else does. Your subordinates are demoralized. Your superiors are impatient to cut their losses, admit defeat, and put the whole thing in someone else's hands. Your credibility is shot. How do you convince everyone involved not simply to go along with yet another scheme you can't prove will work, but to give you more time, more money, and even a bigger chunk of total corporate power?

• • •

When Lee Iacocca took over the chairmanship of the Chrysler Corporation, he stepped into a position experts said would bring him to his doom. The company was reeling under billion-dollar losses. To escape bankruptcy, billions more would be needed to rebuild its gas-guzzling, out-of-date fleet from the ground up. And who wanted to give Chrysler a second chance? "Let Ford and GM take over the market," grumbled some; "Chrysler's too small to compete, and a bailout will only postpone the inevitable." Angry creditors and suppliers were banging on the door; they'd had enough. So had many thousands of Chrysler workers already fuming at massive layoffs and wage and benefit cutbacks. Why should they pay another penny for management's mistakes?

Unfazed, Iacocca launched a one-man communication blitz to rally the company, the financial sector and the nation to his side. He went to Washington and persuaded Congress to guarantee Chrysler a $1.7 billion loan. He charmed, bullied and dazzled suppliers, local governments, private lenders and the UAW into believing that Chrysler could pull through and was worth saving. Then he proceeded to negotiate huge concessions out of every one of them. He persuaded dealers all over the country to carry Chrysler's line despite past failures. He awoke a new team spirit within the mass of remaining Chrysler workers, persuading them to give their all in spite of salary and benefit cutbacks. He raised their morale, made them feel involved in a great cause, and brought new vitality to the company. Finally, he launched a flurry of press conferences and a $200 million TV advertising campaign featuring none other than Iacocca himself extolling his new K-cars, offering $50 to anyone who would test-drive a Chrysler, daring the viewer to prove him wrong: "If you can find a better car, buy one!" The American public was hooked. Rooting for Iacocca all the way, they bought Chrysler stock and Chrysler cars.

Time and again, Iacocca got his message across loud and clear: "Chrysler must be given a chance." He made you believe you had a personal stake in Chrysler, made what mattered to him matter to you.

He won confidence.

He won loyalty.

He won.

And he did it all because, like the understudy who wins front-page raves the day after the star falls sick, he was ready when his moment came.

• Iacocca has known all his life that good communication isn't icing on the cake. It's the meat and potatoes of his profession. "To motivate people you've got to communicate with them," he says. "Otherwise why be in business? Top management should always be reaching out to help the people they're working with, getting them involved, giving them direction, plugging into their needs. Just because you get involved and excited and tear into things doesn't mean you'll die of hypertension next week." Iacocca begins a story: his eyes light up and he rears into action like a race car driver taking the wheel. *He's devoted to communicating 100 percent.* And he loves doing it.

• Whenever Lee Iacocca gets up to speak, he knows just what he wants to achieve and what points he must make to a particular audience. And no matter what questions are thrown his way, no matter how "chatty" or "casual" the occasion, he never goes off track. *He speaks purposively.*

Appearing before Congress to argue for a loan, Iacocca answered questions, but he also scored the points he wanted to make.

"The Treasury Department had estimated that if Chrysler collapsed, it would cost the country $2.7 billion during the first year alone in unemployment insurance and welfare payments due to all the layoffs. I said to Congress, 'You guys have a choice. Do you want to pay the $2.7 billion now, or do you want to guarantee loans of half that amount with a good chance of getting it all back? You can pay now or you can pay later!'" He got his loan.

Though Iacocca was up against the wall in 1979, he communicated like a winner, going straight for what he wanted, focusing attention on those issues he wanted discussed, putting facts into perspective.

• *He knew what he was talking about.* Keeping track of government regulation of the auto industry over the past decade, for example, he could accuse Congress of having acted irresponsibly and support his position with hard facts.

Knowing all there is to know about auto design and market dynamics, he was in a position to persuade all involved that his schemes for putting Chrysler back on its feet were worth investing in. And once the K-car and minivan began to roll off the assembly lines in Detroit, Iacocca was able to sell them convincingly because he knew the value of each design feature, each technical detail, knew what the competition was offering and how it compared to his products. Iacocca's vast pool of information gave him statistics, examples, and illustrations to draw upon at will to bolster his arguments.

• *Well-honed verbal skills* opened his listeners' ears to these arguments, and captured their imagination. Iacocca's style is unequivocally direct, outspoken, bold. It's the style of a man who is strong, honest, gutsy, gritty, real. He describes things with down-to-earth, sensual imagery—the K-car as Chrysler's "gold standard," small cars as "puddle jumpers," the minivan's seat as "fanny-high." His words play on our imaginations. We started seeing Chrysler's cars with Iacocca's eyes, feeling his excitement, saying "yes" to his vision.

He also draws us in with humor. When he appeared on the "Donahue" show and the host asserted: "You're trying to recapture California" with the minivan, he answered: "You're darn right we're trying to recapture California!" Later, returning playfully to that theme, and alluding to Donahue's casting him in the role of the aggressive salesman, he joked: "We'll sell it for $1,000.00 less in California without windows. They go for that out there." After Iacocca had praised the minivan at some length, Donahue interrupted: "Ten minutes for this commercial!" Iacocca retorted: "Well, you let me go on, and I figured since this was a free one I'd take advantage. Usually we only get 30 seconds and we have to pay through the nose!"

• Iacocca works to *cut through* whatever *barriers* exist between him and his listeners by meeting them where they are. During the crisis, he let his workers know how much it grieved him to accede to massive layoffs. "My heart bleeds for those guys," he said, and they believed him. By showing awareness, respect, even sympathy for their position, including their bitterness and disappointment with management, Iacocca *made a strong personal connection* to his workers and forged a new relationship between them, based on mutual trust and understanding. They began to think of him as part of a "we" rather than as an object of suspicion or animosity.

• It's probably obvious by now that Iacocca sold everyone on Chrysler because he sold everyone on himself. Says Maryann Keller, a portfolio manager at the brokerage firm of Vilas/Fischer: "I wouldn't doubt that people have bought a Chrysler car just because they wanted Iacocca to make it." And Ron DeLuca, vice chairman of Kenyon Eckhardt, the advertising company behind Chrysler's TV campaign: "Iacocca has gone from being a corporate spokesman to somewhat of a folk hero." Vince Williams, a Portland, Oregon, auto salesman, opened a Dodge rather than a Pontiac dealership solely because of Iacocca. "All of us at Chrysler believe in the man," says St. Louis plant manager John Burkhardt. "I worship the guy."

The basis of this self-sell is confidence. Iacocca has great self-assurance, even under fire. When he speaks, he does so with such clarity and such a sense of knowing what he's talking about that his listeners have to take him seriously. "With Lee it's almost impossible to win a debate," said one colleague at Chrysler. "He commands you to follow, and you're afraid not to."

• *He's real.* When he says the minivan is "coming on like gang-busters," he means it. He speaks from having assessed his situation as it really is, not as he might wish it to be. If he's up against the odds, he doesn't sugar-coat. Asked if the state Chrysler was in when he took over was as bad as he expected, he says: "You're darn right it was. Worse. It was an absolute mess!" At the same time, he believes in himself and in his product. And he expresses his belief in a way that is more than just "honest." He formulates answers, arguments, explanations in terms that are personally meaningful to him. Describing the Chrysler minivan on "Donahue" he begins: "We're really proud of it. I spent eleven years developing it together with another engineer." This is the real, personal basis of his own belief in the minivan.

He doesn't adopt one voice for addressing the public, another for his workers, and another for government officials, financiers or labor leaders. He may vary the content of his presentations, true, but he always says what he means and does so in the colorful, blunt language that is Iacocca's own. To an audience of college students he said: "You know what? It breaks my heart that I can't say to you today that you've got the world by the tail." To a group of disgruntled managers, it was: "Don't give me any crap!" He connects to each person in a real, flesh-and-blood way, without being either too formal or condescending. And he can do all this, mean what he says, use words that are real to him, relate to others, because he trusts himself.

CHALLENGE #2: MAXIMIZING YOUR CAREER

Are you adept at putting your ideas into words? Do others turn to you to be their spokesperson? Is your voice heard in your organization? Good communicators don't restrict themselves to speaking when spoken to; when they see a point that will make a difference they speak up, never excusing silence with the cop-out that they weren't hired or trained to give opinions on that matter.

Initiating discussions, throwing out thought-provoking suggestions (you don't have to have all the answers), voicing a sharply honed critique: the more actively you enter into the exchange of ideas, formally at office meetings, informally at business lunches, the more valuable you will be. Your stature will increase. Your involvement in business will expand and diversify, and you can build a career that has the shape and scope you choose. In time you may even find yourself explaining company policy to boards of directors, stockholders, the general public or the media, areas you cannot now imagine being open to you.

If this seems like fantasy to you, just take a look at what Millicent Fenwick achieved, largely on the basis of her outstanding skill as a communicator.

An ex-model and associate editor of *Vogue* magazine, Mrs. Fenwick had no professional background in community service or politics when she decided to run for a seat on the Borough Council of Bernardsville, New Jersey, in 1958. As a concerned member of the community and a single parent, however, she had also been involved in local educational reform as a member of the Board of Education. Once on the council, she quickly became a major voice in the community, using her verbal skills to rally support behind a wide range of projects, civil rights causes and prison reforms in particular.

Though she was born into a long-established New Jersey family and educated in exclusive girls' schools, Mrs. Fenwick communicated her concern and compassion so successfully to the underprivileged (seeking them out in person, discussing their needs and problems) that she won the right to represent them. She reached out to the people for whom she fought. And she reached out to the public at large, convincing others to join her in her battles. She made people feel as strongly as she did about these issues.

In 1969 she was elected to the New Jersey State Legislature. Her reputation grew, as did her public profile. (A campaign to provide migrant workers with portable toilets—she was successful as usual—earned her the nickname of "Outhouse Millie.") Elected to Congress in 1974, Fenwick's gifts as a speaker won her influence in excess of that usually afforded a Washington newcomer representing a relatively small district.

Turning her seat into a "bully pulpit," she launched a passionate campaign against governmental corruption. She forced her colleagues to look at both themselves and her in a new light and won a new nickname:* "The Conscience of Congress." Her strong moral sense won Fenwick the ear of the press as well as her colleagues. Said Zbigniew Brzezinski: "She's just damned good. We need a lot more like her."

At the same time, she began to speak out about a broader range of issues. Most dramatically, by speaking on foreign affairs, Fenwick cut a path into that inner sanctum and pinnacle of government power, Foreign Policy. (The achievement could be compared to that of a Johnson & Johnson marketing executive in charge of all the Tylenol accounts for the northeastern United States, daring to discuss international policy with the company's board of directors, and being asked to join the board!) She asked basic questions: How do we choose whom we give aid to? Do we make the politics of a nation's government determine whether or not we let its people starve to death? She spoke so cogently on these points that she was given a seat on the Foreign Affairs Committee (in addition to those she already held on Education, Labor and the Select Committee on Aging), in which she became one of the most active and valuable members.

During debates both in committee and on the floor, Fenwick enhanced the scope and quality of discussion by tossing out new ideas and sharing her thoughts about problems that troubled her. Something in her manner allowed people to discuss explosive issues without exploding. She reminded her fellow legislators of the larger implications of their actions.

*This was actually Walter Cronkite's phrase.

To get people acting and thinking on this level of awareness is leadership of the most creative form.

She was accessible. Her number was published in the Bernardsville directory and she answered calls at all hours of the day and night. She motivated people to be aware of their responsibility as citizens and to make their opinions known on everything from Social Security to U.S. intervention in El Salvador. As Henry Kissinger said: "The task of the leader is to get his people from where they are to where they have not been. The public does not fully understand the world into which it is going. Leaders must invoke an alchemy of great vision."

Millicent Fenwick was reelected to Congress four times, each time by larger and larger majorities. Then, in 1982, after her unsuccessful bid for the Senate (a traditionally Democratic state, New Jersey had gotten caught up in the national reaction against Republican ascendancy in 1982), President Reagan appointed her American ambassador to the United Nations Food and Agricultural Agencies, based in Rome. Millicent Fenwick's abilities were considered simply too valuable to let lapse into disuse.

Her new position is perhaps the most personally fulfilling of Fenwick's career. Through it, she is able to devote herself entirely to the largest and most ambitious of her goals as congresswoman: redressing inequity—hunger, poverty, technological backwardness—on an international scale. It has also opened the door to active involvement in areas of the world she has not yet explored.

As one pictures this indomitable elderly lady kneeling down to comfort an African woman whose baby lies dead of starvation at her feet, or traipsing through a remote village in Ghana, discussing alternative methods of irrigation with a local chief, one feels that Mrs. Fenwick's strength as a communicator will again prove one of her most valuable assets.

From humble beginnings on the school board to world issues at the United Nations! How does she do it? Where does she find the energy and the courage?

• The energy grows out of her belief in *the importance of communication*, of taking a stand, and the exhilaration, for her, of doing what she believes in. "Voice your opinions," she says. "Speak up! The weaknesses of human nature . . . fester and grow in . . . silence and anonymity.

Starting at home, children should hear their parents express anger at violent deeds, pity and shame for the violators of peace and their families." We must speak up, she says, because only then do we have a chance of creating a just and virtuous society.

• Fenwick's courage derives from a strong *sense of purpose*. She never speaks up without having something to say that she feels needs to be said, bringing out a vital consideration another speaker has neglected, shifting the focus of discussion from a peripheral issue to the heart of the matter, arguing with passion when she sees that something must be done. She dares to step forward and interject, interrupt, demand that attention be paid to the injustices she sees: "the [Cambodian refugee] children are so famished they must be fed intravenously before their bodies can accept food." Her purpose is to force us to confront the reality of human suffering and take action.

• Like Iacocca, Fenwick has *an ample body of material* at her command. Whenever possible, Fenwick investigates a topic exhaustively. Before proposing a massive attack on public housing, she did in-depth research to find out why previous housing projects failed. She conferred with architects and met with inhabitants in their homes to find out what they wanted and needed. She personally gathered illustrations of their plight, such as that of an elderly woman climbing up fourteen ice-covered stairs to get home.

Exploring the tragedy of Soviet Jewry, she read personal accounts of their suffering, spoke with their relatives, even traveled to Russia to speak with those involved, both the persecuted and the persecutors.

She has a vast reservoir of facts, anecdotes, quotes and illustrations, an understanding of current events and the nature of government. A voracious reader, Fenwick can quote with ease from history, literature and philosophy. But more importantly, she zeros in on everything around her with a communicator's eyes and ears. Finding the right example to make a point, to persuade your listener, doesn't necessarily come from a reservoir of study, but from a facility for observing and thinking about what you experience. Fenwick's experiences remain etched in her memory, stored up for future use.

• As for her *verbal skills*, they are superb. Her love of words, her years of reading have given her speech a graceful simplicity, an easy eloquence. "I have never seen or imagined such human suffering. The first thought that comes to mind is 'stop the killing.'" She remembers Rabbi Gershon Chertoff quoting to her from *The Wisdom of the Elders*: "Remember, you may never arrive at the solution, but you are never absolved from the responsibility of trying." This, she says, means that "success is not the measure of a human being, effort is."

She can also be earthy. About what she anticipates doing in Africa: "Once you get to a village you go to find the top banana, often some old geezer. You talk to him. You ask him: 'What do you need?' He says, 'Irrigation.' You ask him, 'Where do we start?' He says, 'That field over there.'"

And gritty. "Look around this place [her lawn]. There's not an inch that doesn't have my sweat in it."

Like Iacocca, she has a strong sense of imagery: "The power of the purse, the power of the legislative fist—these are blunt instruments for the delicate operation of diplomatic interchange. It's like trying to open a china box with a crowbar, or untie a knot with your foot."

• Mrs. Fenwick listens to and *identifies with her audience.* She acknowledges that her listeners' thoughts are valuable, and she sincerely believes that opposite views have grounds for common interest. If a speaker communicates in a way that suggests she has all the answers, she doesn't leave space for audience participation or response. The listener feels left out. He may be moved, but he's not moved to action! Fenwick's clearly stated interest in points of view other than her own, her eagerness to learn from others, enables her to reach a lot of people who may not completely agree with her priorities or particular solutions but do agree that the issues are important, that the problems burn. She considers that a triumph. "A good communicator is one who makes you think!"

• Fenwick is *sure of herself as a communicator* because she's not really concerned with herself. The magnitude of what she's striving for lifts her beyond her own situation, helps her focus on what she's saying and why she's saying it. That gives her voice power and authority. Fenwick becomes a sort of medium through which the force of the beliefs that drive her get channeled out to the public.

When you feel this kind of force and power, when you are focused so completely on what you are doing that you almost become it, everything comes together. Losing consciousness of technique, you become like

Yeats' dancer, at one with the dance, or the Zen archer who thinks of nothing but his target, picks up his bow and shoots a perfect shot. The right words just come. You find images, examples, analogies and hit the nail on the head without looking. You soar.

This is what happens to Fenwick, but only because the communication skills she has honed over the years are now so strong that she can forget about them, yet still have them work for her.

• Mrs. Fenwick always *speaks from the heart.* She enjoys her own sense of humor, her stories and quotations. That's why she's able to move her listeners, who can see the sparkle, the indignation or the tears in her eyes. She always begins her presentations with either a personal anecdote or a personal statement, such as "Mr. Speaker, members of the House, we have heard today eloquent statements concerning the barbaric assassination of the former prime minister, the head of his party in a free country. I have family in Italy and this matter is very close to my heart. We should have spoken, too, when the poor policeman in Milan was shot in the back getting into the bus on his way to work."

She talks directly to our senses, our imaginations, our hearts. She shocks us. Touches us. Tickles us. And she feels free to laugh at what tickles her. Once, she made a speech in the New Jersey Assembly proposing an equal rights amendment for women. One of her colleagues rose "with real anguish in his voice, you could tell he was addressing a subject close to his heart, and said: 'I just don't like this amendment. I've always thought of women as kissable, cuddly and smelling good.' [I replied] 'That's the way I feel about men, too. I only hope for your sake you haven't been disappointed as often as I have.'"

She forms an image so strong and evocative that Gary Trudeau used her as the model for his character Lacy Davenport in his "Doonesbury" cartoon. Yet she refuses to romanticize herself. When her campaign manager, John Deardorff, tried to get her to walk past the Capitol on her way to work for a campaign commercial she replied: "I do not walk past the Capitol on my way to work. I don't have time for these games." Deardorff had to make do with footage of her descending into a House office building parking garage.

And throughout any presentation she always returns to her own point of view whether it's with a little segue: "When I was first married..."

or "I don't know how such things can happen. . . ." We always feel she is talking to us, sharing her private thoughts, never that she's making a formal presentation as the representative of a position. She talks as though to a friend: "Let's face it, dear. . ." she'll often say, and it makes us want to see, understand and listen.

CHALLENGE #3: GETTING THE REAL STORY

Just before Gertrude Stein was wheeled off to her last—and as it happened, fatal—operation, her longtime companion, Alice B. Toklas, seized her hand and exclaimed: "Gertrude, what is the answer?" to which Stein is said to have replied: "What, my dear, is the question?"

"One of the key things in business is asking the right questions," asserts Paul Wilson, President, The Mader Group. "The people who ask pertinent, tough, meaningful questions that focus issues do well, and their companies do well."

Do you know how to ask the kinds of questions that keep subordinates, clients and/or experts on their toes? Questions that focus issues and are phrased in such a way as to get specific answers? Questions that pierce through evasions, distortions and generalities, uncover the real facts, divulge the whole story? Get at the problems beneath the apparent problem? How good a *detective* are you?

Can you create the kind of atmosphere (whether one-on-one or on a larger scale) that induces people to open up to you? Gets them communicating freely, honestly, directly? Gets them to reveal themselves? Do you, in other words, *facilitate* communication?

Do you know how to ask the kind of pungent, provocative questions that get people stimulated, enthusiastic, alive with ideas? Do you know how to foment productive interaction and turn a potential confrontation into a cooperative struggle for a win/win solution? In other words, are you a *catalyst*, an instigator?

Finally, can you shape the meetings over which you preside in such a way as to do more than simply "accomplish the business at hand"? Can you, by the way you define problems and goals, connect with larger values that you'd like to have disseminated throughout the organization or department you control: values like the pursuit of excellence, taking responsibility and individual initiative? Are you a *pathsetter?*

To truly excel in the world of business or politics, or any career, you must be able to get to the heart of an event or issue that affects you! Only then can you tackle problems effectively. Only then can you manage crises or make sound policy decisions.

To do all this is to be a communicator in the deepest sense of the word. As Roger K. Smith, Chairman of General Motors, put it: "The truly great executives . . . endeavor to free [their subordinates] and guide them toward developing their own conceptions."

Ted Koppel, host of ABC-TV's "Nightline," is this kind of communicator. True, he doesn't make policy decisions, nor is he responsible for solving the problems he examines. Nevertheless, the communication skills he deploys are so impressive that one reporter, after watching Koppel moderate the New Hampshire debate in the 1984 presidential campaign, said that "Ted Koppel should be running for President!"

Koppel's probing, no-nonsense dialogues with leading experts and notorious figures, statesmen and private citizens involved in some issue of social importance, have won him the ear and approval of intellectuals and policymakers, as well as of the average TV viewer. The media, among them *Time* magazine, the Associated Press, *The New York Times* and the *Los Angeles Times*, have called him "the best interviewer on TV." Comments Jody Powell: "He has the ability to hit pretty hard and get at the guts of something without coming across as offensive or badgering in his manner."

In essence, what Koppel does is to take a single topic on each broadcast of "Nightline" (e.g., IRA Guns: a Cash Controversy, or Herpes and Children: How Great a Danger?) and attempts to find out what's really going on: Why are we doing what we're doing? What are our underlying assumptions? What are the implications of our policy? What objections could be raised, alternatives offered?

Koppel is at once a detective, a facilitator, a catalyst and a pathsetter.

As a *detective*, Koppel manages to get the real story, even when the person to whom he's speaking does all he can to withhold it. The following excerpt from an interview with Pieter W. Botha, president of South Africa, is a study in "how to push in a proper way with a government official who is being deeply disingenuous."

KOPPEL: If you wanted to go to Johannesburg right now...you could get up and leave.
BOTHA: Yes, but it's my country.
KOPPEL: Most black men can't.
BOTHA: Most black men can.
KOPPEL: Cannot.
BOTHA: Can.
KOPPEL: Without permission from the government?
BOTHA: That's right.
KOPPEL: Just leave, go from one place to another.
BOTHA: Yes. Yes.
KOPPEL: Stay there, settle there.
BOTHA: No, not settle there...

Checkmate! No position is exempt from challenge in Koppel's eyes. Consider the following interchange with Roy Cohn, who was appearing on "Nightline" to defend the controversial McCarran-Walter Act authorizing the administration to bar leftist artists and writers from speaking or performing in the United States if their presence should be deemed "dangerous to the public welfare."

KOPPEL: Mr. Cohn, if I wanted to talk to one of these Nobel Laureates, I suppose we could...book a satellite and they come into every American home that chooses to tune in "Nightline" at that particular hour of the evening. So if they can broadcast their ideas here in the United States, what is the additional danger of letting them come in and be here physically?
COHN: I suppose the danger is that it touches off—frequently it touches off riots and other things...
KOPPEL: When is the last time that the presence of an author or an artist or a poet or a composer has touched off a riot in the United States?

But Koppel is more than a crackshot D.A. He is a diplomat. A *facilitator.* He knows how to create an atmosphere that makes his guests feel safe, open up and speak out with amazing, eager candor. "He has," as Frank Snepp, former CIA analyst, says, "the grace and ability to touch something in other people that ordinary reporters can't, and make you feel that he's not merely a reporter but someone who can empathize."

Consider an interview with Christopher Boyce, the so-called Falcon of *The Falcon and the Snowman* fame, now serving forty years for spying for the KGB. At first, Boyce held back. He was reluctant and had difficulty talking. But as he began to sense Koppel's genuine interest in his feelings, Boyce opened up to him.

KOPPEL: Tell me about what it is [espionage] then? Why is it not glamorous? I mean, apart from the fact that if you get caught you end up in the slammer as you did, but what is unglamorous about it?

BOYCE: Well, it's just not what people think it is. It's like picking up a 60-pound stone that you're never going to be able to set down. The KGB is forever. . . .

KOPPEL: Well, give me a sense of—it's an interesting line, the KGB is forever. What do you mean by that? How did it become that for you?

Soon Boyce was revealing with vivid, pointed language what it was like to be a spy. "Espionage is something that grabs you by the stomach and just holds you down and doesn't ever go away. . . . It's like walking into a dark room and falling down a hole." Boyce went on to confess that "I went to them [the Russians] because I was 21 years old and I was so foolish."

And eventually he even drew a moral from his case. "And if the four million Americans with security clearances really knew what espionage was . . . there wouldn't be any espionage. And the government is derelict in its duty if it does not communicate to the four million . . . that fact. That should be done." He himself was communicating so much, so beautifully, that Koppel was moved to say: "Christopher Boyce, I think you've done it, and done it very eloquently tonight."

As a *catalyst* Koppel asks the kinds of questions that stimulate his guests to respond and give. In a group situation, he gets "an electricity going among the participants," as he puts it, while as a masterful orchestrator he keeps the discussion moving forward and focused on the meaningful issues.

An example is one segment of the five-part series on "Nightline" broadcast live from South Africa and anchored by Koppel himself: a discussion between Afrikaner Cabinet Minister Gerrit Viljoen, one of the most powerful whites in office today; Sheena Duncan, the president of Black Sash, a pro-black organization of white South Africans; and Dr. Nthato Motlana, a black physician/activist. Koppel immediately challenged Dr. Viljoen to justify apartheid, while warning him that: ". . . from overseas, it is hard to understand how [these policies] can be justified on moral or ethical grounds. Would you like to try?" To Mrs. Duncan, on the other hand, he suggested that Viljoen's remarks indicated "there is all kinds of willingness to be reasonable, all kinds of willingness to negotiate," thereby getting *her* going. She responded: ". . . negotiations for the destruction of a settled community seem to me one of the most irrational kind of things you could be negotiating about."

Revealing his deep anger toward a ruling class that has so debased his people, Dr. Motlana added: "I've . . . seen movement . . . all of it backwards . . . They're moving the few rights he [the black man] does enjoy . . . These people lost their fertile lands and are now settled in areas where they cannot produce anything."

Under combined pressure from both Duncan and Motlana meanwhile, Viljoen's careful facade of tolerant good will began to crack, laying bare a strong undercurrent of impatience and resentment toward black South Africa: ". . . where . . . a chief is appointed . . . in the traditional fashion and then confirmed by the government, he's considered to be a puppet because he was not elected. But in the case of the elections . . . people refuse to participate and then . . . consider themselves to be the authentic leaders . . ."

Resettlement, pass laws, issue after issue was explored in-depth by the three leaders, with the same level of intelligence and passion. For his part, Koppel remained primarily a catalyst, once he had gotten things truly under way. I was once told by a labor negotiator that "the secret of arbitration is to know when and how to get out of the way, and let the process happen." Koppel did that but from time to time, he stepped in playing devil's advocate, offering insights of his own, citing facts, scoring points first for one side then the other, so neither would be overwhelmed, and each had a fair chance to state his or her case clearly. Ultimately, however, he got them to express their grievances openly without putting words in their mouths. In this way, the real dynamics of the South African conflict began to make itself dramatically visible, including the serious lack of trust and perceptual distances between the Afrikaner government and the black leadership, as well as the emotional forces at play: the rage, frustration, bitterness and fear that are tearing that nation apart.

As David Halberstam put it: "Koppel unveiled South Africa's troubled soul."

What is so remarkable is that Koppel fosters the kind of dialogue that reveals much, without the dialogue itself breaking down. Equally striking is the way this pathsetter can open up a dialogue by leading his guests to consider the subject under discussion in terms of important questions or underlying issues they might not have broached on their own (or even been aware of).

Consider the following interchange with Atlanta Mayor and former U.S. Ambassador to the United Nations Andrew Young vis-à-vis Jesse Jackson's personal diplomacy in the Middle East. (Jackson had recently flown to Syria on his own initiative to "negotiate" the release of Navy Lieutenant Robert Goodman. Welcomed enthusiastically by President Assad of Syria, he returned victorious, but debate raged over whether the then presidential candidate had acted from humanitarianism or political self-interest.)

KOPPEL: Mayor Young, let's sharpen the focus a little bit. Humanitarianism, sure, why not; political motives, who doesn't [have them]; but what about the business of a private citizen engaging in foreign policy?...

YOUNG: ... the decision-making process in the State Department requires about 17 different clearances before a diplomat can get his talking points. . . . I just ignored them, frankly, and I think any success I had was due to that. . . .

KOPPEL: Well, if I hear you correctly, what you're suggesting then is, as far as diplomacy is concerned, scrap the State Department and let's all go our own way and do the best we can.

What Koppel does here is to shift the focus away from the Jackson/Goodman incident as an isolated event, and zero in on the general question it raises: Should a private citizen take it upon himself to engage in state business without official authorization? What kind of precedent is Jackson setting no matter how honorable his intention? And what sort of attitude toward legally sanctioned organs of power like the State Department do his actions suggest?

In the final analysis, Koppel is an educator. He educates himself, he educates his audience and he educates the people he interviews by challenging their assumptions (Roy Cohn), their values (Gerrit Viljoen and Andrew Young) and sometimes simply by making them feel that what they have to say matters (Christopher Boyce). Under the best circumstances, his guests leave with a more acute perspective and enhanced awareness of the problems with which they're involved.

Koppel's formidable expertise as a communicator enables him to cover any issue or event with equal finesse, even a story that has just broken one-half hour before he goes on the air. In fact, he is at his best when the going gets tough and he's called on to cover an on-going crisis as it unfolds day by day. Untangling complexities, separating rumor from fact, honing in on key issues—he does all within the context of a rapidly changing and enormously confusing situation. His coverage of the Iranian hostage crisis (1979–80) and the Americans held hostage in Beirut in 1985 prompted *Wall Street Journal* reporter George V. Higgins to write: "Ted Koppel is a most outstanding 'crisis manager' ... he functions most effectively when things are at their worst."

In a world rife with surprise takeovers, terrorism, and catastrophes on the scale of Union Carbide's Bhopal disaster, what professional can afford not to be able to handle crises effectively?

Although the nature of Koppel's work is quite different from Fenwick's and Iacocca's (he asks questions, they answer them), his effectiveness can be traced back to the same basic attributes.

• Like them, *he is devoted to what he does.* "I love doing 'Nightline,'" he exclaims. "If someone said create for yourself a program that is the quintessence of what you would like to do ... I would have a hard time coming up with anything more than I have. When other kids wanted to to be firemen, I wanted to be Ed Murrow. What could be more exciting than having a chance to talk every night for a half hour to the greatest experts in the world? 'Nightline' ... is my dream job."

• *He has clarity of purpose and approach.* Although he doesn't write his questions out beforehand—because, as he explains, "If you come in with just your own questions in mind, you may find that the person you are interviewing says something interesting and you may ignore a very good follow-up question"—he does have a vivid sense of what he wants to get out of the interview. Just as a businessman attends a meeting with a clear agenda in mind, a sense of what he wants to get out of that meeting, Koppel comes to the anchor desk each night knowing what he wants to cover, what he's interested in finding out during this particular broadcast. That's what gives his discussions direction and focus.

In a program on DPT (the legally mandated anti–whooping cough injections to which an unknown number of infant deaths have been attributed) Koppel's purpose is to find out what a concerned parent would want to know: Why hasn't the AMA come up with an alternative? Are alternatives available elsewhere? What are the risks involved? With that sort of agenda in mind, Koppel keeps the discussion moving forward while staying free to dip into whatever happens at the moment or follow up as needed.

• *Koppel's knowledge is power.* It is a knowledge that comes from twenty-three years' experience as a top ABC reporter under his belt. And like Fenwick, he's voraciously inquisitive. In addition to reading at least six major newspapers a day and preparing for his program, Koppel keeps track of all the major news broadcasts. He is constantly probing, questioning the information he absorbs. (Hearing that General Motors just recalled half a million cars, he exclaimed: "It's the most extensive and expensive recall they've ever had. What goes on at GM when this happens?" and scribbled a note to himself.)

His broad knowledge gives Koppel the wherewithal to make his questions and objections specific and rigorous. Challenging Dr. Viljoen on the South African government's right to even consider resettling blacks, he asserts: "—why should people who had land deeded to them by Queen Victoria's government, who have been on that land with that kind of authorization for certainly the last 80-some years . . . why in heaven's name should they be moved at all?"

• *Verbal skills.* Koppel has the ability to formulate his questions and comments in plain, concise, clear English. William Lord, vice president of ABC News, credits this facility with enabling Koppel to "re-ask and rephrase his questions, and not let [his guests] go on a quick and simple answer."

In one of the segments on South Africa, Koppel interviewed journalists Percy Qoboza and Otto Krause, and Dr. Beyers Naude, a white leader in the anti-apartheid movement. Koppel asked Dr. Naude why he had suddenly converted from a strong racist position to a supporter of the black cause:

DR. NAUDE: I came to the conclusion . . . that . . . apartheid was un-christian, it was immoral, and it was unfeasible. . . ."

KOPPEL: Mr. Krause, is the policy of apartheid justifiable on moral and religious grounds, do you think?

MR. KRAUSE: I think that one cannot look at these things solely in moral or religious lights.

KOPPEL: I'm not asking you to do that. I'm just asking you whether it can be justified on those grounds.

MR. KRAUSE: I think it can very much be justified. . . . But the point is that what is necessary in this country . . . is growth. . . . And this is a matter of a country raising up all its people, uplifting them in standard of life . . . we are doing this job. . . .

KOPPEL: All right. Here we have Percy Qoboza, a man who was a Niemann fellow at Harvard—I suspect he doesn't need any more uplifting, at least intellectually. Your response, Mr. Qoboza, to the notion that the white man's burden in this country is to lift up the blacks.

Koppel used the most precise words to phrase his question, making it very difficult for Krause to avoid a direct answer.

Even his on-the-spot retorts come out in complete grammatical sentences, unmuddied by "uhm's" and "uh's." When at the outset of a discussion of cold-war politics William F. Buckley began criticizing television's journalistic integrity, protesting: ". . . how is it that American television feels that we can be informed . . . by listening to the paid propagandists of the Soviet Union?" Koppel suggests that if Mr. Buckley answers the questions put to him on television, the American people will be informed.

Not only are his questions and comments extremely clear, they're almost always phrased in such a way as to help the interviewee get right to the point. In a one-on-one discussion with former President Carter, Koppel did not generalize: "What do you think about present Mideastern policies?" but instead specified: "... you were ... critical of the strategic relationship ... between the U.S. and Israel ... Why?" He didn't ask: "How do you feel about moving the American embassy in Israel to Jerusalem?" but "[A] Why is that such a Key issue and [B] ... why do you disagree?"

Koppel's command of language includes a sense of humor that plays freely on well-worn sayings and phrases: "Gentlemen, you're in danger of talking over everybody's heads but your own." "On that minor note of agreement let us take a commercial break." It's a subtle but powerful tool which helps break down his guests' defenses and transform potentially unpleasant confrontations into constructive and honest exchanges.

• Probably the most important quality Koppel has as a communicator is his masterful way of *listening*. There's an extraordinary attentiveness about him, a highly developed capacity to focus completely on the person he is interviewing. "You have to keep the antennae out," he insists. "You have to try and sense how your guests are feeling. Are they in a humorous mood? Are they in a belligerent mood? Do they want to get involved in a fight, and if they do, and if that fight is going to be a useful means of exchanging ideas, then you encourage them. If it's just going to be a couple of people nose to nose yelling at each other ... then you have to nip it in the bud."

Koppel's own antennae are excellent. He knows how to listen *actively*—asking himself all the while what the communication he's receiving implies, questioning, probing. This, more than anything else, is what permits him to get on a wavelength with his guests, and hear the hidden message beneath their words. The nine years Koppel spent as a diplomatic correspondent taught him how to read between the lines and understand the subtleties of what was being said, especially when the person speaking was trying not to say anything.

What is more, he listens not just to confirm what he already thinks, but to find out something new. He's open. Interested. Eager to learn. Willing to hear the truth even if it's different from what he would have expected. "As a journalist you have to listen. You are not imposing your own opinions, you are listening to opinions exchanged by others. What you have to do is be careful not to rush to judgment because there really are other points of view."

This attitude not only helps Koppel reveal the key issues behind the story. It helps him become part of a "team" with his guests. Although he is not an active participant imposing his own opinions, he is "in there with them," struggling to grasp what they are saying as they struggle to express themselves clearly. His listening galvanizes the interview into a dynamic give-and-take.

People tend to open up more easily to Koppel because his listening shows a respect and a desire to hear what they have to offer, whether it's the expertise of a former president of the United States or the simple experience of an auto mechanic. He is human and keenly sensitive to their positions.

This humaneness comes through most clearly when he's dealing with victims of social outrage or political oppression. We feel a real warmth in him, an enormous delicacy and tact, but one that is absolutely without pity or patronization. Unlike so many interviewers whose attitude of "I understand how much you've suffered" is a bit too easy and smacks of condescension, Koppel seems to know that he *can't* understand what these people have gone through, that all he can do is try to feel it. In this way, he grants them their integrity and their dignity. By openly admitting to the difficulty he has in addressing their pain—as he did with the Hiroshima survivor Mrs. Shibama to whom he said: "Was it painful for you to see that film [*The Day After*] or—I don't quite know how to ask the question." His vulnerability comes through. Then, too, he can ask terribly painful questions and not be offensive, because he does so with an acute awareness of the pain involved. To Mrs. Shibama, for example: "Then please tell us, what is in your heart, what is it that you want people to know about those days—"

"If you are listening to find out, then your mind is free, not committed to anything; it is very acute, sharp, alive, inquiring, curious and therefore capable of discovery," wrote Krishnamurti, the Indian philosopher.

It is this kind of listening which encourages, and gets responses for Ted Koppel.

• *Confidence.* "Ted is the most self-confident man I've ever met, and I've met a lot of people, including Henry Kissinger and Charles de

Gaulle!" says Barrie Dunsmore, colleague and friend of Koppel's for twenty-five years.

He is not afraid to intrude when necessary: to call someone on evasions or deliberate lies; to demand more precise definitions; to cut in when one participant in a discussion becomes overbearing or goes on and on, and to do so firmly and directly. At the same time he is sure enough of himself never to allow irritation to get the better of him. If someone insults him, he's able to let the provocation slide. If one guest proves impossible to reach, he goes on to the next. He doesn't need to prove anything about himself, or keep himself in the spotlight.

In his book *The Savage Mind*, French anthropologist Claude Lévi-Strauss describes two ways of approaching any situation. One way is that of the technician who has learned a formula for dealing with a finite set of situations. If he's confronted with an unforeseen situation or doesn't have the right tools on hand, the technician is at a loss.

The other way is that of the *bricoleur*. He is flexible, dealing with each problem as it arises on its own terms and using whatever tools are handy. If he doesn't have a hammer to nail two boards together, he'll pick up a stone and use that. Sustained by his confidence, Koppel is the *bricoleur par excellence*. He builds his questions out of what the other person gives him and uses the other person's language and behavior to tell him how to proceed. This is true interaction, communication in its highest form.

• Ted Koppel is *real*. In loving what he does, being truly interested in the issues he addresses and addressing those issues from his personal background and experience, he brings his unique self to bear in each segment of "Nightline." He reasons things out using his common sense and intuition, and he asks questions to which he is truly interested in having an answer.

I'll never forget how struck I was by Koppel asking a disabled athlete: "... is it ever an advantage to you just to have one leg?" The same question had been on the tip of my tongue, but I would never have asked it, feeling it to be crude or insensitive. Yet when Koppel asked it, it came out of a sequence of ideas and acceptable logic.

"If you are watching some guy hop up to a high jump, and here is a man with only one leg, and he is about to jump 6 feet 8 inches, which is something 99.9 percent of the public with two legs could not do, all of a sudden the thought comes to you: 'Well, wait a second, he's carrying less weight, right? He's got one less leg.' I don't think there's anything improper or rude or stupid about asking that question."

As the orchestrator of the action, his personality takes second place. Yet in the way Ted Koppel orchestrates that action, his own personality does come through. And that is what being real is all about: being true to the action you're involved in, true to yourself and true to your response to the world around you.

We have talked about how three excellent communicators use their skills to meet challenges and achieve success. Their styles are vastly different: Lee Iacocca, the bold businessman; Millicent Fenwick, the cultivated public servant; and Ted Koppel, the detective/facilitator. Yet they have much in common.

- They love to communicate, perhaps because it is their way of sharing their unique gifts.
- They have a purpose, and they believe in that purpose. Also, their reasons for speaking are generally larger than themselves.
- They know what they are talking about. And they've made the information they've gathered their own.
- They have good verbal skills. They use images, aphorisms and humor to give clarity, directness and earthiness to their language.
- They know how to connect with their listeners. They make the person they're talking to feel acknowledged. Their communication is two-way: it invites give-and-take. It elicits a response.
- They have confidence and control.
- They are real. They are comfortable with who they are. They don't try to play a role.

These are qualities you too can possess. They do however take time to develop. Success rarely hits you like a moonbeam and transforms you. You need to commit yourself to the challenge of taking one step at a time as these three communicators did. At the beginning of his career Iacocca recalls: "It wasn't easy. I was bashful and awkward...and I used to get the jitters every time I picked up the phone. Before each call I'd practice my speech again and again, always afraid of being turned down." Ted Koppel had been working at his craft for seventeen years when he became host of "America Held Hostage" in 1979. He was not ABC's ideal choice of an anchorman, but his superb ability to communicate turned the network management around in his favor and convinced them to keep him on the air. Millicent Fenwick began her career by communicating at informal meetings, school board meetings and the New Jersey House of Representatives before tackling her biggest challenge—Congress.

In my work as a coach, I've seen that once people begin to practice the method set forth in these pages, they experience significant and exciting changes. Even a few weeks of practice can make a dramatic change.

The basis of everything you will learn in this book is what I call "being real." When you are real, you are there, responding to your listener, sharing your own thoughts and associations. *Becoming* real is a process. It is a constant, a continuum, yet an ever-changing element of successful communication. It's what makes you unique.

Chapter Two

THE KEY: BEING REAL

At every moment you choose yourself. But do you choose *your* self? Body and soul contain a thousand possibilities out of which you can build many **I**'s. But in only one of them is there a congruence of the elector and the elected. Only one—which you will never find until you have excluded all those superficial and fleeting possibilities of being and doing with which you toy, out of curiosity or wonder or greed, and which hinder you from casting anchor in the experience of the mystery of life, and the consciousness of the talent entrusted to you which is your **I**.

—Dag Hammarskjöld
Markings, 1964

Your real self, with all your experience, insight and strength, is the most valuable resource at your disposal. If you use it wisely, after making a presentation, interviewing for a job or negotiating a raise, you will be left with a very special feeling. You won't feel as though you have only shared information with your listeners, you will feel that you have shared yourself with them. And if they believe in you, they will believe in what you have to say.

Success as a communicator, in fact, depends on how much self you allow your audience to see. You must present that self as authentic and important—what I refer to as "real."

"That man is absolutely for real! He got to me." At rock bottom, this is the sort of response every person in the public eye—be he or she lobbyist or diplomat, businessperson or politician—must go for. If achieved, true effectiveness, believability and impact—all will be won. But while many people, especially in this era of media consciousness, feel the need to "do something" about how they come across, most believe that this means hiring a public relations firm or an image consultant to create a persona for them. This is a mistake, just as misguided as delegating all responsibility for your text to a speechwriter.

The invent-an-image method does not work; witness any number of politicians who hire consultants to mastermind their campaigns. They are taught how to dress and how to sit, given cue cards to read from and little lectures about "smiles" and superficial "eye contact," external devices aimed at making them look "natural." All they end up looking like is stiff, detached robots. You can't create humanity from the outside in.

We live in the era of the "global village." Television has brought the starkest reality into our living rooms—the assassinations of John Kennedy and Anwar Sadat, war atrocities in Viet Nam, John Glenn launched into space, Neil Armstrong walking on the moon, and U.S. citizens held hostage in Iran and Lebanon. We have been witnesses to all these. As a result, lifeless or artificial presentations no longer make the grade. Whether on television or in front of a group, communicators today must project their real selves if they're going to have any impact on sophisticated TV-conditioned audiences.

To project your real self, you must do so from the inside out, in terms that mean something to you. Also, you must respond to how you uniquely experience thoughts and sensations. If you are really thinking, you can maintain that train of thought, say what you want to say in an organized fashion and at the same time be flexible enough to have your thought broken and return to it. People who know what they are saying can absorb an interruption very well. In other words, you must react honestly and flexibly to whatever happens to you while you talk (questions, har-assment, laughter and so on) and be able to deal with these things while maintaining a previously arranged structure to your communications.

As one of my most brilliant and receptive students, the late Jessica Savitch, anchorwoman for NBC, put it: "I find the best way to be an effective communicator is to be what you are on the air as well as off the air. . . . Viewers will respond positively if you are real. They don't know—there is no sign that comes up over your head saying 'this woman is real, this woman is not a fake,' but it is a *visceral* reaction. Somehow when you are yourself, you become three-dimensional instead of two-dimensional."

Three dimensionality, being in touch with real feelings, at one with your body, reacting honestly and humanly to the world—these qualities make the successful communicator stand out.

So what do you do? Where do you go for the persona that will draw people to you? How do you present your *self* to the public so as to win them over?

You trust that self. To get at what is involved in such trust, consider for a moment a notion I first came across in my acting career.

BEING PRIVATE IN PUBLIC

Lee Strasberg, the famous acting teacher whose students included Marilyn Monroe, Dustin Hoffman and Robert de Niro, pointed out that what people really want to see on stage is the actor being private in public. I think that is exactly what audiences are moved by, whether at a play, a speech or an event of world importance televised live. They want to experience real people.

When you read a book, listen to a piece of music, watch a sunset or think about something important to you in the privacy of your own home, you get in touch with your truest self. When you are moved, your thoughts, feelings and associations flow uncensored. You cry, smile, wince without even thinking of how you are coming across. In other words, you respond intimately and openly to whatever you are experiencing. Being private in public means tapping that sensitivity and intensity within.

In his book *Robert Kennedy and His Times*, Arthur Schlesinger, Jr., describes a speech Kennedy gave in an Indianapolis ghetto the night Martin Luther King, Jr., was shot. I'd like to quote Schlesinger here because he so effectively captured how stunningly and courageously real that speech was.

> It was a cold and windy evening. People had been waiting in the street for an hour. . . . They had not heard about King. Kennedy climbed onto a flatbed truck in a parking lot under a stand of oak trees. The wind blew smoke and dust through the gleam of spotlights. "He was there," said Charles Quinn, a television correspondent, "hunched in his black overcoat, his face gaunt and distressed and full of anguish." He said: "I have bad news for you, for all of our fellow citizens and people who love peace all over the world, and that is that Martin Luther King was shot and killed tonight." There was a terrible gasp from the crowd. . . . "Martin Luther King dedicated his life to love and to justice for his fellow human beings, and he died because of that effort. . . . For those of you who are black, considering the evidence there evidently is that there were white people who were responsible, you can be filled with bitterness . . . or we can make an effort, as Martin Luther King did to understand and comprehend and to replace violence, that staining bloodshed that has spread across our land, with an effort to understand with compassion and love. For those of you who are black and are tempted to be filled with hatred and distrust . . . I can only say that I feel in my heart the same kind of feeling. I had a member of my family killed. . . . But we have to make an effort in these United States. . . . Let us . . . say a prayer for our country and our people."

Kennedy admired King. He felt his death personally, the more so because it recalled the death of his own brother. His pain was unmitigated and profound; yet instead of trying to hide this anguish he spoke from it. He allowed himself to be private in public. In addition, however, Kennedy cared deeply about the black underclass and this caring gave him a sense of purpose. He allowed himself to be vulnerable, the more dramatically so because he didn't know what their reaction to King's death would be, and because the police refused to protect him in the midst of the crowd.

Whether as a statesman grappling with the agony of a terrible tragedy or as an executive announcing the closing of a plant, allowing yourself to be private in public is the essence of being real.

You need not feel that Robert Kennedy's depth and achievement are out of your league. If you look to yourself to express your inner life, as Kennedy looked to himself, true communication can result.

There is a method you can use. It involves three processes:

Relieving Tension
"Being Alive"
Developing Sensory/Emotional Awareness

RELIEVING TENSION

Tension is the greatest barrier to becoming real. To understand this, try to move a piano or lift a two-hundred-pound weight, and in the midst of the effort ask yourself: "What is 702 times 4?" You'll find that you can't think because your whole being is locked up in trying to move the weight. The same holds true when you are tense. Tension impedes concentration and stops the natural flow of your senses, so you can't focus on speaking freely. Tension traps your energy.

How can you learn to relieve tension?

Clear your mind of distractions, particularly of urgent business back at the office, so that you're not bringing your desk with you to the speaking situation.

Concentrate on what you're going to say for ten or fifteen minutes beforehand, without anyone else's intrusion. This is particularly difficult in a luncheon or dinner situation, when the people at your table want to make conversation. Still, it's perfectly acceptable to either excuse yourself for a few minutes or politely state that you must review your notes during dessert and coffee. If you choose the latter, just sit quietly and let the conversation flow around you.

Let go. After you've reviewed your remarks, sit quietly and concentrate on releasing tension from your forehead, eyes, mouth, neck and shoulders. If you have any specific areas of tension, concentrate doubly hard on them. Say to yourself, "Let go, ease up." Once you've perfected this technique, you'll find that even your breathing will change, a sure sign that you're relaxed and ready to go to work.

"BEING ALIVE"

Oral communication takes place on many levels. Words are important, unquestionably, but to make those words provoke, excite, sting or comfort another person, you must be keenly aware of what the text means, both to you personally and to your listener.

Relate to What You're Saying

"I cannot sell a painting unless I think it has an artistic value," a New York art dealer told me recently. "Even if I know it will be a good investment for the buyer, I have to believe in it as art to make an honest case for it."

That kind of commitment to product or service creates conviction. When what you talk about is important to you, conviction and belief come automatically.

Recall Lee Iacocca's commercials. The company's survival was on the line, as well as his own. And when he said, "Chrysler's cars will be better than other cars because they *have* to be," he convinced us he would make them better, single-handedly if necessary.

Sometimes, though, you have to *work* at uncovering why the material is important to you. Here are two helpful rules:

1. Learn everything you can about your subject. The more you know about it, the more excited and passionate you'll become.

2. As you learn, ask yourself: "How does this relate to me?" "Do I care?" "What does this mean to me?" For example: "The disease of muscular dystrophy, which I am discussing with this group, could it strike my little girl?" Or, "The beautiful car I am presenting to this customer, would it make my own family happy?"

If you are handed a pre-designed presentation, complete with slides and text, you need to make it your own. Tell the story as you see it and experience it. If you're given slides, put them in a sequence you feel will get the message across.

IBM executive Jim Cassell tells this story about himself:

"Back in 1972 when I had to give a presentation to 4,000 people in Cobo Hall in Detroit, Michigan, I went to the arena to check it out beforehand. I even practiced the carefully written-out speech IBM wanted me to give with a tape recorder so that I could give it exactly as written. After it was over, I couldn't remember a word I had said, or how it went. I was paralyzed with fear during the whole thing.

"Eight years later I had to give a presentation in Cobo Hall again, but this time I did it my way. Instead of a speech that was written out word for word, I used an outline. I knew what I wanted to say, having thought it through and made it my own. I practiced, but I wasn't trying to please a boss, or anyone but myself. I was much more real and spontaneous. I even enjoyed giving the speech."

Relate to Your Audience

To communicate with your listeners, talk *with* them and not *at* them. When you recognize and absorb your listeners' reactions, an electrical circuit is sparked between you. There is an energizing give-and-take. Smile if the response pleases you. Show a touch of hurt or anger if necessary. If you see confusion in the eyes of the person you're talking to, clarify. *Acknowledge the reality of your relationship to your listeners.*

Much more will be said about give-and-take in chapter 5, "Practice and Delivery." For now, just be aware that these interactions create a vital bond between you and your audience.

During our school years, there was for many of us one teacher who made an indelible impression on us. That teacher cared, gave of herself, and helped shape our lives.

There is a "learning need" inside each one of us. If you can care about the people to whom you are speaking with the intensity and rapport of a teacher who cares, you will trigger that need. You'll establish a connection, as all successful communicators do.

Relate to Your Surroundings

You must also be sensitive to your physical environment. Be aware of the lighting, the temperature, the "atmosphere" of the room. Is it cozy and inviting or sterile and cold? The way you sit in a chair, lean across a podium or notice the flowers on a colleague's desk plays a part in defining who you are to the people around you.

Sometimes things go awry, but if you are tuned in to your surroundings, you can actually take advantage of the surprise factor.

Johnny Carson is a master at handling the unexpected. No matter what goes wrong he incorporates it into his show. One night, Carson had a guest on the "Tonight" show whose act included a singing parakeet. The bird simply would not sing and the trainer was in danger of falling flat on his face, bringing the show down with him. But Carson turned the bird's silence into a joke far more entertaining than the original act could have been. "Well, I think we might just have to eat this bird," he deadpanned at one point. The audience howled.

When you handle distractions and mishaps with grace or humor, you set your listeners at ease and create a more intimate relationship with them. You take the audience into your confidence. When you *fix* something that's gone wrong right there in front of the audience, your listeners feel they are, for an instant, transported "backstage." You are truly private in public, human.

Relate to Yourself

If you are aware and responsive to your words, your listeners and your surroundings, then you will be in touch with yourself.

Consider the great violinist Itzhak Perlman. Perlman seems overpoweringly physical. His face reflects his own reactions to the sounds he is making. Sensation, thought and emotion flow through him. During a TV performance I watched his face in close-up. His expression went from a twitch to a kind of snarl, from a heavenly smile to an impish grin, to pain, laughter, sadness, surprise. Throughout it all, sweat was pouring off his nose—and you could see him feel it.

Paradoxically, communication is achieved as a result of awareness of self. Being in touch with himself makes Perlman's music transport the listener to faraway worlds. So, in order to move people, you not only reach out to them, you stay in touch with yourself. Being there, being at one with yourself and your own physical, sensory reality is the essence of "being alive."

But you can't learn how to connect with your material, your listeners, your environment or yourself simply by reading this section. It takes time, practice, relaxation and use of your senses.

LEARNING SENSORY/EMOTIONAL AWARENESS

We experience the world around us through our five senses—sight, hearing, smell, taste, touch. It's one thing to know intellectually that people are listening, but only when you see their faces, and hear them laugh, grumble or applaud do you really connect with them.

Yet seeing and hearing are by no means the only senses. The remembered taste and smell of salt air can make you experience a day at the beach more immediately than any picture can. Helen Keller, who lived her entire life both blind and deaf, makes us realize how much we miss by ignoring the feel of things: "My body is alive to the conditions around me," she wrote. "The rumble and roar of the city smite the nerves of my face, and I feel the ceaseless tramp of an unseen multitude, and the dissonant tumult frets my spirit...."

Developing the Senses

Just as muscles can be developed, all five senses can be developed.

When I was in acting class, we spent weeks and months honing the quality of our five senses. We would, for example, try to re-create a sensory experience like one of these:

Smell	Garlic
	Perfume
	Garbage
Sight	Sunset
	Dead Animal
	Ocean Waves
Sound	Church Choir
	Fire Engine
	Bird Singing

Touch	Block of Ice
	Baby's Skin
	Thorns
Taste	Chocolates
	Castor Oil
	Tobacco

After you have relaxed, and released your tension, imagine touching a block of ice. Try to re-create its temperature on the palm of your hand and fingers, its wetness, its texture. Or imagine a baby and run your hand over its face. Experience the delicate texture, its velvety quality, its warmth. Don't consciously try to show or indicate a reaction on your face. If you are practicing smelling garbage, for instance, don't try to grimace. Don't think about what your face is expressing at all. Concentrate on the sensation alone. The more patient and gentle you are with your senses, the more they will reflect what you are experiencing.

Sensory Recall

If your senses are sharpened, not dulled with tension, you will automatically connect to your material, your environment, your audience and yourself. But to make sure your presentation will "live" under any circumstances, structure your remarks so they are sensorially provocative to you. Make what you say appeal to your senses. This gives both you and your listener triggers with which to create aliveness.

For instance, we know a lot of money and technical expertise are involved in making a television commercial. The goal is to make the viewers' mouths water when a good orange juice commercial is presented. In a similar fashion, your words can stimulate your listeners' senses and your own. Hearing you, the listeners experience in a visceral way whatever you are talking about.

When she returned from the Sudan, Barbara Bush spoke of a child she had held in her arms who was seven years old. He weighed the same weight as her seven-month-old grandchild. The impact of that image left an indelible impression.

A remembered event lives in our ears, noses, fingertips, throats, eyes. You don't remember your child being sick with fever as an abstraction;

you remember stroking her damp hair with your fingertips, feeling her burning forehead on the back of your palm, hearing the sound of uneven breathing and of blankets swishing as she tossed about, smelling the vaporizer's fumes filling the room. The past comes flooding back in torrents of sensory impressions. Indeed, the more profoundly moving a past event is, the more vividly it will express itself through the senses.

Jacqueline Kennedy described the President's assassination less than a week after the event:

"There'd been the biggest motorcade from the airport. Hot. Wild. Like Mexico and Vienna. The sun was so strong in our faces. I couldn't put on sunglasses. . . . Then we saw this tunnel ahead, I thought if you were on the left the sun wouldn't get into your eyes. . . . They were gunning the motorcycles. There were these little backfires. There was one noise like that. I thought it was a backfire. Then next I saw Connally grabbing his arms saying no, no, no with his fist beating. Then Jack turned back so neatly, his last expression was so neat . . . you know that wonderful expression he had when they'd ask him a question about one of the ten million pieces they have in a rocket, just before he'd answer. He looked puzzled, then he slumped forward. He was holding out his hand . . . I could see a piece of his skull coming off. It was flesh colored, not white—he was holding out his hand—I can see this perfectly clean piece detaching itself from his head. Then he slumped in my lap, his blood and his brains were in my lap. . . ."

Theodore White writes: "She remembered, as I sat paralyzed, the pink-rose ridges on the inside of the skull, and how from here on down (she made a gesture just above her forehead) 'his head was so beautiful. I tried to hold the top of his head down; maybe I could keep it on . . . but I knew he was dead.'"*

The almost clinical detail of this description is amazing. But Jacqueline Kennedy's emotions and their effect on us are far from clinical. Indeed, it is because Mrs. Kennedy's experience was so traumatic and the depth of her reaction so profound, that she could relive it through all her senses. And with this reliving, she makes us feel the full tragedy of her loss.

*Theodore White, *In Search of History* (New York: Harper and Row, 1978), pp. 521–22.

Use the Technique of Emotional Recall

The first time you speak on a subject that is deeply moving to you, your message will most likely come across powerfully. But if you have to make several appeals to Congress, say, or rehearse a TV public service announcement twenty times, you may find the emotional juice running dry. Then you may need to use an emotional recall exercise. This exercise was created and developed by Lee Strasberg of The Actors Studio.

Think of a traumatic experience you have lived through—the infidelity of a loved one, the death of a child, a stinging personal failure. It should be several years old so that it is deeply implanted in your psyche.

Once you've pinpointed an experience, try to re-create the sounds, smells, sights, tastes and touches associated with the event: the beep of a car horn in the street, the steady downpour of rain, the touch of a loved one's hands against yours. Experience these memories with your senses rather than intellectually. Search for them. Talk the exploration out loud. Don't rush. Let the recall of the senses take over. You are creating these sensations, so you are in control.

Here is an example of how I go about the exercise, step by step.

I sit in a chair, relax and let tensions flow out of me. I start recalling whichever sense comes to the surface first. In this instance, I begin with touch. (There's no need to speak in complete sentences.) "I'm wearing ... it's rough, alligator, brown little slits in them..."

When one sensory image has been thoroughly explored, I go to another: "The air is... my throat is dry, nostrils... the smell is old, musty, choking my throat... the bottoms of my feet hit the soles of my shoes, I feel the slap, the rush, slap, go, sting, rush, body, chest hard, air stifling, hard to breathe, go, go, rush... I see him... soft, white hair, eyes bloodshot, thin, smooth cane, textured spring coat, beige hat, felt brim, gray, sharp, quick, lips on my face, eyes red, watery, expressionless..."

There is no need to create a story line or narrative. Your experience will be private in nature, so there's no need to reveal it. The sensory awareness is key. But to help you understand the process, I will tell you that the above emotional memory did concern a traumatic experience of mine. At the age of twelve, I was late getting to the train station, and barely made it in time to say good-bye to my father. It was the last time I saw him alive.

As you do the exercise and speak the words out loud, connecting to and experiencing your sensations, the incident you are re-creating takes on a life of its own, and you feel deep emotion.

The purpose of the exercise is to reawaken the senses, so that at the appropriate moment, in a speech, in a meeting or whenever you choose, you can be moving and *real*.

I found that I could use the emotional memory I experienced in several plays. I used it while playing Anne Sullivan in *The Miracle Worker*, in a scene that called for me to beg Helen Keller to keep trying and not be overcome by frustration. I had to keep spelling words into her "mute" hands, reaching for some sign that she understood. In another play, *Hogan's Goat*, I used the exercise at a key moment when I confronted my husband with my shame for not being legally married in the eyes of the Church. So far in my speaking career, I have not made an impassioned plea or been in a situation where I needed that emotional recall, but I'm ready for it should it occur.

This is how an effective actor can create reality while repeating the same text for eight performances a week. This is how, in a crucial speech, you can call on your own resources (in this case, your senses) to make the dramatic or poignant moment happen.

Your senses are the tools of your craft as a speaker. If you learn how to use them, then everything—your tone of voice, your choice of words, all facets of the way you speak—will be real, and moving.

Use Literature

If you find it hard to re-create sensory and emotional responses through such exercises, don't despair. The feelings within you are there. Every individual has a rich personal reservoir of sensory and emotional memories, but sometimes this treasury is difficult to tap. Here literature can be of great help, for there is practically no emotion or sensation that fine writing has not beautifully evoked.

Read a passage you find especially moving. Immerse yourself in the sensations and emotions it arouses. Then close the book and continue creating the sensations and the images evoked. You can even do this right before a speech, "warming up" just as an actor prepares off-stage before making an entrance.

If you are giving a speech, consider using a moving quote from literature. John F. Kennedy and Winston Churchill were famous for this. For example, Kennedy, addressing the joint session of the Dail and Deanad Eireann, Dublin, Ireland, June 28, 1963, said: "George Bernard Shaw, speaking as an Irishman, summed up an approach to life. 'Other people,' he said, 'see things and say 'Why?' But I dream things that never were, and I say, 'Why not?'"

Winston Churchill's sense of Old Testament retribution was evident in his judgment after the London blitz: "They have sown the wind; let them reap the whirlwind."

Use Real Objects

One Gulf & Western executive I know was giving a talk on the various applications of zinc, exhorting his listeners to buy the metal even though its price was high. At a crucial point early in his presentation, he asked his listeners to reach under their chairs. Mystified, the participants did so and found, taped to each chair, a small container of zinc vitamins. The executive spoke about the valuable properties of zinc, how it "improves your sense of smell and your sexual prowess, and removes white spots from your fingernails." They were a delighted and attentive audience from then on.

Real objects used skillfully in a presentation will engage the audience by appealing to their senses of sight, touch, smell, taste and/or sound.

VULNERABILITY

On a "Donahue" show several years ago, Eleanor Smeal, president of the National Organization for Women, felt she was losing the debate to her opponent, Phyllis Schlafly, whose language skills and smooth delivery techniques seemed more effective than hers. But at a critical moment Smeal turned the situation around. Schlafly kept refusing to answer a question put to her by Phil Donahue concerning the Right to

Life Movement's proposed amendment to prohibit the use of IUDs for birth control. When Smeal called her on that, Schlafly retorted by describing Smeal's face as that of a woman who wanted to kill and continue killing a million unborn babies a year. In a husky but calm and steady voice Eleanor Smeal replied: "You know, I was raised a Roman Catholic, and this issue is very important to me, very important, because I *had* to practice birth control. . . . I happen to have a disease called Mediterranean anemia. Mrs. Schlafly has six children. I probably wouldn't live if I had six children. . . . I don't like saying this on national television . . . but I think we should treat this situation seriously, because it is a serious issue."

Smeal's sensitivity to what she felt was an intimidating attack made her response meaningful and powerful for many women. At that moment the tide turned in the St. Louis auditorium. The audience supported her. Having been open and vulnerable, Smeal relaxed and grew stronger in the debate. She confronted Schlafly as she had never done before.

Being real means that at times you may have to be vulnerable. However, I don't think of that as a negative quality. It can be a positive thing in communication, as it was with Eleanor Smeal. When you are able to acknowledge a sense of vulnerability within yourself, you can win the hearts and respect of those around you. People will empathize with you because everyone has at one time or another been in a vulnerable position.

The following story shows how another person allowed his vulnerability to surface. Along with time, energy and commitment, it helped him develop into a "real" speaker.

John Sculley's reputation preceded him, and I was intrigued by the prospect of working with the forty-five-year-old dynamo who was then the chief executive officer of Pepsico and is now president of Apple Computer, Inc. A slightly built but powerful man, he had developed a considerable reputation among his colleagues as a charismatic speaker.

"Wait till you see him. He's dynamic, he's poised. He really knows what he's doing."

What I saw, in fact, was a man who reminded me of the way great orators of the past had spoken: he strode about the stage making dramatic pauses, and carefully timed his gestures to coincide with certain theatrical effects, such as an American flag dropping from the rafters during his conclusion. Impressive, yes. Personally compelling, not quite. Something was missing. Given his intelligence and his commitment to his company, I felt he could have done much better.

When we met in my office, we began by viewing a videotape that Sculley had brought along. He wanted me to help him look more at ease on camera.

"What do you think?" I asked him when it was over.

"It's forceful," he said confidently. He was right. There had been power in his voice, and energy in his body. I went to the next question.

"What would you like to improve upon?"

"I look a little stiff," he responded. "I could be more conversational."

"Did you make your point? Was your message clear?"

"Not specifically enough."

I suggested we look at the written script and mark it for clarity: underlining the key words, circling the key thoughts, enumerating the points leading to the climax, and so forth. After we did this, John spoke the text into the video camera and microphone. We played it back. The improvement was evident. He was more direct and his message came through more potently.

But still, something was missing. So I decided to give John the exercise I usually reserve for the third or fourth session with a client—Interpretation of Literature. He was to choose a literary passage which moved him. He opted for a passage from William Agee's *A Death in the Family.*

After reading it through silently, he spoke the passage out loud to me. About two sentences into the text, his voice broke and the words began to come out choked and haltingly. Finally he couldn't speak at all.

"I can't go on," he said quietly. Confronted as he was with a passage that moved him as deeply as this one did, his voice simply stopped working. The connection was intense.

I too was moved. It is always a poignant moment when I see someone connect with their deepest, innermost responses for the first time.

"What happened," I explained to John, "is that you touched a deep chord within yourself. In time you'll learn how to express a deep response verbally without choking. Still, what you let me see here involved more of your real self and grabbed me more than anything on those videotapes."

At the end of the hour, John Sculley knew, not just intellectually, but through personal experience, that there was much more of himself available for use as a real communicator.

After that first session, which Sculley called a "consciousness-raising experience," he decided to broaden his commitment to become a better communicator. We worked on several skills—relaxation techniques, vocal variety and body language—but we always came back to that seminal experience with *A Death in the Family*. We used it as a continuing "connection" to get all his presentations to matter the way that reading had mattered.

The first major test of our work came five months later. Pepsico was holding a national convention in Las Vegas to mobilize all its bottlers in a confrontation the company considered crucial. It was fighting a 1971 ruling of the Federal Trade Commission that declared that the seventy-five-year-old tradition of allowing soft drink companies to set up exclusive franchises resulted in a restraint of trade and was therefore illegal. If the decision stood, the bottlers would not only have to compete against bottlers of other soft drinks but against companies trying to bottle Pepsi as well. Many of the bottlers would have been driven out of business.

Rather than allow the traditional system to be disrupted, Pepsi decided to fight the government. John Sculley went around the country talking to bottlers, inspiring them to fight the ruling in Congress. It was a decisive moment for his company and he needed to communicate as effectively as possible. The Las Vegas convention would be the climax of the mobilization campaign, and John Sculley was to be the principal speaker.

It was a grandiose affair, replete with onstage elevators two stories high, a marching band and numerous special effects, including a trapeze artist. Two thousand people were in the audience. If there was ever an opportunity for all our preparation to pay off, this was it.

At the appointed moment, John Sculley strode out on the stage with confidence and poise. His gestures were in sync with his text and his voice was free to respond to what was going on inside him, and a *lot* was going on.

He knew what was at stake, what the battle meant to him and to his audience. And even though the lights were bright and he couldn't see the audience, he didn't talk *at* them. He talked *to* them, as individuals with the same stakes, the same hopes and fears. He dug deep down into himself as he had done with *A Death in the Family*. Only now he was able to control the choking.

John Sculley didn't try to be as "big," or theatrical, as the twenty-foot-tall, three-panel slide presentation projected behind him, or the fifty-piece band that played "America the Beautiful." But he was big; he held his audience spellbound because he spoke to them from within. He let them see how much he cared. He let them see who he was and what he stood for. The speech was a success. The convention was a success. The Pepsi Cola Bottlers Association worked hard and convinced Congress to kill the restrictive legislation.

You may be thinking: "I'm not John Sculley. I don't have his talent, commitment or expertise." Perhaps not, but you have reserves of emotion and energy that you too can learn to tap whenever you want to express yourself. Thousands of my clients who are not CEOs or public figures have followed the methods described in this book and made stunning progress. The changes take place gradually. Even the so-called "naturally gifted" communicators practice for years to hone their techniques and become real. As Margery Williams wrote in *The Velveteen Rabbit*:

> "What is REAL?" asked the Rabbit one day.
> "Real isn't how you are made," said the Skin Horse. "It's a thing that happens to you."
> "Does it hurt?" asked the Rabbit.
> "Sometimes," said the Skin Horse, for he was always truthful. "When you are real you don't mind being hurt."
> "Does it happen all at once, or bit by bit?"
> "It doesn't happen all at once," said the Skin Horse. "You become."

PART TWO

ALL YOU NEED TO KNOW TO GET YOUR MESSAGE ACROSS

The Lilyan Wilder Program
(Steps One–Three)

Chapter Three

ORGANIZING YOUR THOUGHTS

(Step One)

To profess to have an aim and then to neglect the means of its execution is self-delusion of the most dangerous sort.

—John Dewey
Reconstruction in Philosophy

Being real is your foundation as a speaker. Though a look of effortlessness is your goal, it takes hard work to achieve that look. Being real is not the same thing as being "natural." If, during a sales presentation, for instance, you showed your "natural" enthusiasm for your product only by gushing and exclaiming "It's stupendous!" you would not be very persuasive. To be effective, your enthusiasm must be backed up by a strong, well-worded argument.

A sportscaster who came to me for coaching had fallen into the "being natural" trap. He was upset because the producer of his show had asked him to use good grammar and organize his thoughts. "They want me to be natural," he complained, "but when I talk like myself, or use 'ain't,' they say, 'No!'"

His producers were right. The sportscaster started designing his presentations for clarity, taking into account the needs of his audience. The self that began to come through was not his "natural" unprepared self, but the self that was there for the purpose of communication. He now uses good grammar, and can answer such questions as: "WHAT do I have to say? WHY am I doing this piece? HOW am I going to present it?"

In this chapter you too will learn how to design a presentation so that it is both articulate and "the real you."

CHOOSE AN OBJECTIVE

Whether you are going to be making a thirty-second toast or a thirty-minute speech, you begin by asking yourself what you intend to accomplish. All effective communication tries to influence other people, to make them think differently, act differently, support a cause, buy a product, laugh, get angry or find new hope.

What do you want your remarks to do?

What do you want from the people you are addressing?

The answers to these questions will give you a clear sense of purpose, an objective.

Sample Objectives	Desired Response
To negotiate a book contract with a publisher that will win you, the author, the greatest support and exposure.	A great contract.
To sell your bank's C.D.s	Customers purchase them.
To raise money for cystic fibrosis research.	Contributions.

Choose an objective that is simple, clear and achievable. Formulate this objective in a single sentence: "I want to...."

Arouse Instinctive Drives

"The roast pigeon won't fly into your mouth!" advises an old proverb. To accomplish your objective, you have to move your audience. This means appealing to one of the four basic drives that motivate all human beings: survival, ego, pleasure, altruism.

The instinct for *survival* is the strongest instinct of all. We care about the arms race, the economy, jobs and taxes because any one of them can threaten our lives. Politicians routinely address themselves to the survival instincts of voters when they campaign, as do certain activists— Ralph Nader and Helen Caldicott, for example. But even a junior executive appeals to his boss's survival instinct when, in presenting a proposal, he makes it evident that his ideas will strengthen his boss's stake in the company. Self-preservation is a universal need.

The need to maintain one's *ego* is also extremely important. Tap this drive by appealing to your listener's ambition and pride.

What I'm about to describe is an unusual event, but it illustrates how people's sense of themselves, their egos, can be tapped for a worthwhile cause.

On July 13, 1985, upwards of 60 rock stars donated their talent to a "Live Aid" television concert to benefit Africa's starving masses. The response was overwhelming both in terms of dollars (approximately 70 million) and the human "fellow-feelings" it provided.

Those who saw the concert, 92,000 in the JFK stadium in Philadelphia, Pennsylvania, and about the same number in Wembley Stadium in London, England, plus over a billion television viewers, were proud to be part of an event of this stature and excitement. Our egos identified with and were inspired by the rock stars who performed. "If they could give of their time and talent, we could be there, and contribute money," we thought.

Though you and I need to motivate on a smaller scale, we too can use our listeners' desire for identity, status and recognition to accomplish our goals.

The drive for *pleasure* makes us crave sex, good food, vacations, Giorgio Armani suits. A superior hi-fi salesman won't just show potential customers his new quality equipment; he'll appeal to the pleasure principle and make their ears tingle!

Altruism provides us with a fourth motivational drive. If you ask a neighbor to contribute money to the Fidelco Guide Dog Foundation (and you're not a rock star with whom he wishes to identify), you're appealing to his sense of altruism: "These German shepherd dogs are well bred, trained on the blind person's premises, and given to blind people for a nominal fee. Certainly this is a worthy cause that needs your attention."

Try to find ways to motivate your listeners throughout your presentation. It will keep their responses flowing.

ANALYZE THE SITUATION

Look at the speaking situation from all angles and answer these four questions.

To Whom Are You Speaking?

How much do you know about your listeners? What do they know about your subject? If you are trying to sell someone a car, find out if he or she knows what fuel injection is before launching into a pitch on the marvels of the Bosch-J Tronic injectors.

According to Millicent Fenwick: "You've got to be responsive to the audience. If they seem puzzled by something, you've got to expand on that before going on to something else."

Robert Kennedy was keenly attuned to his audiences. But he did not defer to them. He didn't don the work clothes of a grape picker when addressing the United Farm Workers, or start using Chicano slang. Simply knowing their experiences, "he could see things," said Cesar Chávez, "through the eyes of the poor. It was like he was ours."

Who Else Will Be Speaking?

When possible, learn as much as you can about rival salesmen, co-negotiators, other speakers on a panel, etc. If you find out in advance who they are and where they stand, you'll be able to anticipate rebuttals, challenges and questions, and plan your remarks so they don't echo those of another speaker.

When the discussion follows a specific order (e.g., in a panel situation) find out what the order of presentation is. If you are first, it will be up to you to break the ice. If you aren't first, what kind of act will you have to follow? An excruciating bore? A rival with eighty researchers at his disposal? Or a brilliant wit whom you couldn't dream of topping? The secret in this third case is: Don't try! Vice President George Bush, following on the heels of Art Buchwald at a benefit banquet, knew he could never be as funny, but he could be charming and persuasive by simply being himself.

You can't always know everything about the people you're dealing with; I merely suggest that you try to get as much information as you can to enhance your presentation.

What Is the Occasion?

Find out all you can about the occasion. How formal is it? How much time do you have? Is this a once-a-year meeting where you'll be expected to make a twenty-minute presentation, or is it a weekly rap session with more flexibility and range?

If you are up for an interview, is it one-to-one or will you be facing a panel of four?

Where Will It Take Place?

As part of your planning, consider where you are speaking. When appropriate use humor, personal reminiscences and historical references about the place to add flavor to your presentation. For example, in the shadow of the Lincoln Memorial, Martin Luther King, Jr., said: "Five score years ago, a great American, in whose symbolic shadow we stand today, signed the Emancipation Proclamation...."

Adjust the tenor of your remarks to the environment. In a church, make sure your language, images and references don't clash with the solemnity of the surroundings. In a bare, unadorned meeting room, use humor: "We didn't want you to be distracted by the scenery." Outdoors, refer to the weather, the landscape or even urban blight if this is what surrounds you!

Once you have determined your objective, your listeners' motivations, and analyzed the situation, you are ready to plan your thoughts.

PLAN YOUR THOUGHTS

While conducting a seminar for a group of managers at a private bank, I asked each participant what he wanted to achieve during our two and a half days of developing communication skills. Five out of eight wanted to learn how to "be in control." Fortunately for them, they had something to be in control of—content.

Concerning yourself with how you come across, with being "in control" or "conversational," are empty goals without first taking into account what you want to say, and how you're going to formulate your thoughts so that they connect to your listener. Without substance, style is superficial.

Finding Materials

Most people who are good at communicating work at it all the time. They are inveterate clippers of magazines and newspapers, keeping files of quotations, statistics, biographical data and transcripts.

To decide what materials will actually go into your presentation, ask yourself these three questions:

> Does this clarify what I'm saying?
> Can my listeners relate to it?
> Does it excite me?

If you're dealing with current technology or financial statistics, it's essential that your information be current. Robert Metz, managing editor of the Financial News Network, works to keep ahead of the business news. At a presentation he made for the Food Marketing Institute, Metz was making changes and checking statistics even as he rode up the elevator to the meeting room.

Using Tools

Lay your thoughts out on paper by either talking them into a tape recorder and then transcribing them, or by writing them out, sketching them in outline or note form. There's no one right way; do whichever is best for you.

Complete your first draft as simply and quickly as possible. If you stop and fuss too much the first time through, you may lose the flow of your language and thought. This flow is vital. If you get stuck on a particular point, move on and come back to it later.

As you edit your presentation, cut and paste. Next to paper and pen, scissors and tape are the communicator's most valuable tools. If what you've put on paper doesn't seem to flow properly, cut each thought into a strip and try arranging these strips in different order, like a collage. Nine times out of ten you will see something visually you would never have hit upon by rearranging the same thoughts in your head.

As you approach a more final version, you might also paste your pages onto a wall or a board. That way, you can get a picture of your presentation as a whole, determining at a glance if you have given your points their proper weight.

Deciding on a Length

Find out what maximum time has been allotted to you, then settle on a length. Make your points quickly! Your boss is more likely to promote you if you save him time than if you weigh him down with an excess of detail. Even on more formal occasions, advises a top-notch political speechwriter: "Keep your introduction short, your conclusion short and leave as little as possible in between!"

Use the following table as a guide, keeping in mind that it is somewhat arbitrary because each situation is different.

Kind of Presentation	Length
Toast	1–2 minutes
Award acceptance speech	3–5 minutes

Serious, in-depth speech (makes about three major points)	15–20 minutes
Remarks and/or answers at an interview	15 seconds to 2 minutes
Sales talk	3–10 minutes
Presentation to the boss	1–10 minutes

Select One Main Point

Boil your thoughts down to *one central message.* If you bombard your listeners with too many ideas they won't absorb any of them. Give them one big, clear idea they can really sink their teeth into. Note: Within one central point you can make subsidiary ones, as we shall see, but you need that main theme or message, tailored to accomplish your objective, to pull your presentation together.

For example, a doctor running for mayor of a medium-sized city was preparing to deliver a major campaign address and simply could not decide on a central theme. As a result, the speech he showed me went all over the place and was bound to leave his audience confused. I asked him, "If you could leave your audience with only one thought, what would it be?" He immediately answered, "I'd tell them that as a doctor I am a healer; as a mayor, I want to heal the city." His message had been there all along; he just needed to pin it down. He returned to his speech and reorganized his points around that one theme.

Now you have a reservoir of back-up information, a length and a main point. You are ready to enter into the final stages of organization and give your presentation structure and style.

STRUCTURE

In its final form, your presentation should have an Introduction, Body, Climax and Conclusion.

The Introduction tells the audience what you're going to tell them.

The Body tells them.

The Climax clinches your main point.

The Conclusion tells them what you told them.

For practical reasons it is usually best to prepare your presentation in a different order.

Begin by structuring the *Body*. This is the heart of your presentation and will naturally lead you to the Climax, the Conclusion and, lastly, the Introduction.

Here is an example using the structure described above.

In negotiating a job transfer from Detroit, Michigan, to New York City, the manager of a beauty salon enters the boss's office (with this skeletal outline) and says:

[THE INTRODUCTION]

Good morning, George. You were terrific in the marathon yesterday,. Have you recovered? . . . Thanks for taking the time to see me today. I need to cover four important areas with you about managing the New York salon.

They are:

1. What I've done in the past.
2. What I can do in the future.
3. What my personal and professional needs have been in Detroit.
4. What my personal and professional needs will be in New York.

[THE BODY]

First, as you well know, in Detroit I've built a strong staff with the depth that will allow us to help strengthen the other North American units. The team is loyal, morale is high and the salon is profitable.

Second, I can build a caring, trusting rapport with the staff while at the same time evaluating them for proper positioning. I'm able to establish the sense of security necessary for the foundation of a well-run salon.

Third, my mobility rests upon the liquidation of my condominium in Detroit and I would appreciate any advice you may have. The approximate costs involved in moving me will be. . . .

Fourth, in order for me to move laterally and maintain my present standard of living, this is the financial package I need. . .

[THE CLIMAX]

Without sounding self-serving, let me tell you that I feel I'm the best person to manage the salon in New York. That salon's bottom line is the result of an insecure, unstable staff and I can turn it around.

[THE CONCLUSION]

So—now you have a better idea of:

What I've done in Detroit.
What I can do in New York.
What my needs are in Detroit, and
what I'll need in New York.

I am really looking forward to the challenge. I want to go all the way for our company, like you went all the way in the marathon. How does what I've outlined strike you?

The structure of this example can be repeated on any number of occasions. But what if you expect to be in a situation where there will be a lot of give-and-take? "How can I plan an introduction, body, climax and conclusion in advance when I don't know what will come up when?" you may ask.

I advocate what I call the "*minispeech*" to guide you when you need to present information in more flexible situations.

The minispeech is a structured approach to whatever your speaking situation may be. If you depend on another person's questions and contributions to determine the flow of your remarks, you are putting that person in the driver's seat. Go into every encounter prepared to be a one-man or one-woman show!

Oprah Winfrey, talk show hostess of WLS-TV's "AM Chicago," was invited to be on the "Tonight" show with hostess Joan Rivers. I suggested she prepare her remarks in the form of a minispeech: "Know your objective. Ask yourself why you're taking that long trip to California." Oprah prepared. When she got to the studio, she found that everything was scripted for both herself and Joan Rivers, but that Ms. Rivers did not follow a word of it. Oprah was stunned: "I was waiting for Joan Rivers to ask the questions. I saw that she had the script in front of her, but she ignored it. So, I started talking."

Oprah started by describing her upbringing ("little white girls were 'spanked,' I was 'whupped'"), the reason for her overweight ("I ate a lot") and her work as a talk show hostess ("I'm going to Ethiopia in three weeks"). It all came rolling off her tongue in a wonderfully funny, exuberant and moving way. Her presence enhanced the show tenfold, because she brought her minispeech with her and was fully prepared.

Familiarize yourself with your minispeech as completely as possible. If you're knocked off your course, or rattled by an unexpected question (or no question at all), recall its structure. Use it as a guide to get back on course and maintain control.

Now let's move on to the actual shaping of your speech, or remarks, by beginning with the Body.

Developing the Body:
Tell Them

After determining your objective and central message, select two or three subsidiary points to support your central message. When possible, make a numbered list—the three-point program, the four reasons, etc. The mayoral candidate who wanted to present himself as a healer developed his theme by saying he planned to:

1. Rebuild the inner city, so his constituents would have decent homes in which to live
2. Shape up the city's health services, particularly the hospital emergency wards
3. Go at crime tooth and nail, so people could feel safe in and out of their homes

Organizing your material this way focuses your listeners' attention and helps them remember your message later on. If reporters are present, they will pick these points out of the speech for their own stories.

Next, choose one of the six following formats to link your points together:

The Topical Format presents two or more aspects of a program, phenomenon or theory. The mayoral candidate used the Topical Format.

The Chronological Format links your points together sequentially in time. The first event goes first, the second goes second, and so on. A recipe instructing you to (1) beat eggs, (2) heat a skillet and (3) pour the eggs into the skillet would be an example. So would the three steps of artificial resuscitation, the four stages of the French Revolution, or the six phases of a two-year program to salvage corporation X.

The Comparison or Analogy Format describes one program or phenomenon in terms of another. For example, this year's marketing plan in terms of last year's marketing plan (goals, strategies, costs);

> The goal we set for ourselves last year was to expand our sales and distribution apparatus, and we were successful. This year our target is to achieve greater sophistication in our sales approach. [goals]

> We plan to do this by setting up a series of regional sales conferences to plan a national campaign that will take into account the unique requirements of each different territory. This will replace the one national meeting and one campaign approach of last year. [strategies]

> We were limited in our sales strategy last year by strict cost eliminations, but this year we can spend more because of the gratifying increase in overall revenue. [costs]

The Mixed Time-Frame Format takes stock of the *present*, flashes back to the *past* to explain "how we got here," and then sweeps forward to a vision of "what lies in store," the *future*. Here is an example taken from a speech delivered to college graduates:

> President Reagan may have made optimism fashionable by clinging to it and articulating it at a time when Americans were in a receptive mood. But in our own city and state—where many of you will pursue your careers—the forces of a positive attitude are bearing remarkable fruit. [present]

> Lord knows Detroit and Michigan went through some truly profound economic miseries during the last recession. . . . Michigan has been an industrial giant through most of the century. [past]

Well we're on the road back . . . bringing business back to Michigan.
. . . Detroit is building again, growing, exploring new ideas and working
to regain its status as a premier convention city. [future]

—"Information, Gateway to Success"
Beverly A. Beltaire,
President, PR Associates, Inc.
Warren, Michigan, May 10, 1985

The Problem-Solving Format makes three points: (1) what you want
to do, (2) what the opposition wants to do, and (3) how your plan is
better than theirs. An example is President Reagan's address defending
his proposed budget for 1983:

[Point 1] Not only must those deficits be reduced, they must show a
decline over the next three years, not an increase. Our goal must be
a balanced budget.

[Point 2] Apparently, the philosophical difference between us is that
they want more and more spending and more and more taxes.

[Point 3] There hasn't been too much opportunity in the last 40 years
to see what our philosophy can do. But we know what theirs can do.

The Gestalt Format informs the listener with an overwhelming barrage
of facts, statistics and quotes. Instead of limiting the number of points
you make to strengthen your central message, in the gestalt speech you
multiply them to include as many as you can. The audience doesn't
come away from this sort of speech with one central point in mind, but
rather with a strong, visceral reaction.

An example is Dr. Helen Caldicott's speech against nuclear arms
buildup:

Today America has between 30,000 and 35,000 hydrogen bombs . . .
both countries have enough to overkill every person on earth about
sixteen times . . . every person would be vaporized, turned into gas . . .
concrete would burn . . . there would be decapitations, traumatic organ
injuries . . . millions of shards of flying glass and steel, objects hurled
against people, and people hurled against objects . . . a fire storm would

spontaneously ignite . . . there would be no people to come to help because they would all be dead.

Caldicott was unrelenting, bombarding us with fact after fact, image after image. At the end of the speech the audience may not have remembered a single specific image, but there had been an aggregate effect.

Developing the Climax

The climax, for both speaker and audience, is a moment of release, or catharsis—the moment when the audience experiences: "I get it! You've made your point!" Whether it is met with a hush of silence, gales of laughter or thunderous applause, your climax is the real clincher, the moment of payoff.

It generally comes at the end of the body or in the conclusion. Arrange your thoughts in increasing strength so that they move to a peak of intensity. You can do that by (1) setting the background or (2) stating the points which lead like stairs up to the climax. No better example exists than the brilliant conclusion of the Martin Luther King "I Have a Dream" speech.

Developing the Conclusion:
Tell Them What You Told Them

"This is the way the world ends," T. S. Eliot lamented in "The Hollow Men"—"not with a bang, but a whimper."

I try to get my clients' presentations to end not with a whimper but a bang! Your conclusion should be attention-getting and compelling, pulling everything said into sharp focus and driving your message home. Resist the temptation to keep talking.

The Summary Conclusion tells the listeners what you told them. For example, a Group Product Manager in charge of the Tylenol account could end his report on promotional strategy to an executive staff meeting as follows:

To sum up, we're initiating a two-pronged campaign to go after the Extra-Strength Tylenol business. One, we have a TV campaign aimed at the trade which will establish pressure there, and two, we have a promotion planned for the consumer involving coupons, rebates and discounts.

The Motivational Conclusion appeals to higher values, the ego drive or powerful emotions such as pity, fear or compassion.

Speaking to a group of AT&T salespeople on how to improve corporate efficiency, Michael Sherlock, executive vice president of NBC, ended with an appeal to the egos of the audience:

So we end where we began, with you. With the individual performance. That's what excellence is all about.... The pay-off is financial, sure. But more than that, it's a personal sense of satisfaction at a job well done, a job that counts.

The Application Conclusion suggests concrete steps the audience can take to follow up on what you've told them. "Go home and write your congressman," you might say, or "Call this number and pledge $15 or more to help combat cerebral palsy," or "Go back to your desks and put the 'Blueprint for Action' kits to use."

The Dawn-of-a-New-Day Conclusion is meant to be inspirational. Grant Tinker, president of NBC, concluded a pep talk to the NBC affiliates:

You've been promised a rose garden before, and you've gotten mostly weeds. I'm asking you to have faith in one more promise. We need each other, and together, we have nowhere to go but up. If you believe, we'll meet here at the Century Plaza a year from now, and... we will springboard that day from a different word. Gone will be "inertia." We will be dealing with "momentum." Look it up.

Developing the Introduction:
Tell Them What You're Going to Tell Them

With your climax and conclusion all worked out, it's time to go back and work out an introduction. There are three requisites. You need to:

Seize attention. Use a provocative attention-getting tactic to attract your audience right off the bat. CBS Anchorman Charles Osgood told me he always tries to begin by playing off the meeting's "running gag":

> I went to Denver for a two-day seminar to speak before a group of money-managers. When I asked the Program Chairman how long he'd like me to speak, he said: "As long as you like, but I hope you won't speak as long as Louis Rukeyser did last year." It turned out he had talked for two and a half hours. "I have fourteen points and I want to make them all," he said. As he proceeded to deliver the talk, I was told, at table after table, people got up and left. There were only a few people left at the end. So when I got up to speak I said: "Good afternoon. I have ten points to make." They all knew what I was talking about.

This is but one of many attention-getting tactics. In a section called "Highlights" starting on page 97 of this chapter, you'll find others.

Establish rapport. You may use one or any number of the following suggested tactics. These are just guides. There are infinite ways to establish rapport, and you will no doubt discover tactics all your own. You might:
- Graciously acknowledge the introduction given you
- Refer in a generous way to something someone said
- Make a joke about yourself. Julian Gibbs, the late president of Amherst College, began one speech as follows:

> When I received the invitation to speak at your commencement, I asked Mr. Williams to give me some advice about my speech. He said: "There are three things to remember: keep it brilliant, keep it witty, and keep it short." I said: "You're asking an awful lot." He said: "Well in that case just forget the first two."
>
> I'll try to follow his advice.

- Express a sincere feeling of pleasure. You can comment on anything from your listeners' civic concern to their recent accomplishment as a work team. Just be sure to mean what you say; false compliments are easy to detect!

• Tell an anecdote inspired by the place or occasion. History doesn't move us as much as a current association: "Everytime I come to Cooperstown to talk to you, I feel a pang of regret for not having pursued a career in baseball."

• Work with the special interests of your listeners. One of my students knew that her boss loved chocolates. When she arrived to ask him for a raise, she presented him with a box of Godiva's. "But you must open it now," she said. When he did, he found a typed memo outlining what she intended to cover during their meeting. "The real chocolates come after you've heard me out!" This particular boss loved the humor and the chocolates. Caution: not every boss will.

• Refer to an idea of an event which is of dominant concern to your audience. On the day Robert Kennedy was shot, the daughter of a friend of mine was graduating from high school. No one knew if the senator was going to survive. Two or three fathers in the audience had worked personally with Kennedy, and were crying openly. Rising to speak, the headmistress paused for a moment, then began:

> We all mourn the tragic event that took place this morning in Los Angeles. I seriously considered cancelling today's ceremonies in view of what has happened. But finally I decided against this. Senator Kennedy would want us to proceed. He was a firm believer in the power of education to change the world, to curb violence, to spread compassion and understanding and so, in his spirit, let us continue here today.

In trying to establish rapport, a problem can arise if there is disagreement between you and your audience. Acknowledge it openly, but be sure to maintain a good-humored, sportsmanlike tone. James C. Miller III, then FTC chairman (currently Director of the Office of Management and Budget), once spoke about government regulation of health care before the aggressively anti-regulation Oral and Maxillofacial Surgery Political Action Committee: "It's a pleasure to be here to discuss with you the FTC's activities in the health care field," he began. "After hearing this, some of you may question my sanity, but surely you won't question my courage!"

Tell your audience what you're going to tell them. This is the third important element of introductions. Franklin Roosevelt began one of his Fireside Chats by saying: "I want to talk for a few minutes with the people of the United States about banking. . . . I want to talk to you about what has been done in the last few days, why it has been done and what the next steps are going to be."

Let's look at an example of how one speaker managed to accomplish all three goals within a single opener. The speaker: California Governor George Deukmejian (then state attorney general). The subject: crime in California in 1980.

> Today in California you are four times more likely to be the victim of a murder, four times more likely to be the victim of a robbery, and three times as likely to be victim of a rape, than you were in 1960.
>
> Facing as we are this criminal crisis in California we have to give some thought to how we can best reduce the crime on our streets and by reducing that crime, allow every citizen the freedom to live in safety and happiness.
>
> The best way to reduce crime is to prevent it before it happens. More resources need to be put toward this—the front end of the criminal justice spectrum.

(1) Deukmejian leads off with three eye-opening statistics to grab the audience's attention. (2) He establishes rapport by relating to the community. And (3) he talks about what he will talk about: the problem of escalating crime and how to solve it.

STYLE

Two words sum up the most important thing you need to know about style. *Be yourself.* If that sounds too easy (or too hard), keep in mind three specific ways to help you "be yourself."

First, *use your own language.* Many people have the notion that a presentation ought to sound formal or different from real talk. They tend to sound like the embodiment of a cause or an institution instead of like themselves. When I ask them: "Is this what you really want to say?" they invariably answer: "No, here's what I mean..." and in their own words, make their points beautifully.

Begin with those words.

Second, while you plan your remarks, *imagine yourself talking to a close friend*. This is the way FDR organized his fireside chats. He made millions of Americans feel as if they knew the President personally and could trust him as a friend. "I hate war, my wife Eleanor hates war, and even my little dog Fala hates war," he said once.

Third, *use your own personal kind of humor* to say what you mean. Humor doesn't mean planted jokes but an overall good-natured approach to life which leads one to chuckle, smile or even sigh at an ironic truth.

Try to follow these guidelines. If you do, your personality will reach and touch your audience.

Clarity

Before anyone can be affected by what you say, he must understand you. Clarity of expression is the essence of good communication.

First of all, *use good grammar*. If you don't know a particular rule, look it up. (A good reference is Strunk and White, *The Elements of Style*.) Thoughts grammatically expressed line up in the listener's mind with the order and neatness of pearls on a string. Bad grammar tangles the string so that your audience has trouble seeing just how the pearls align. Remember, though, you're writing for the ear and not the eye. Certain points of grammar can and should be relaxed in favor of more idiomatic usage. Recall how Winston Churchill made wry fun of a common taboo, not to end a sentence with a preposition: "It is the sort of nonsense up with which I will not put."

Second, *simplify your language*, especially if you're dealing with a highly technical subject. No thought is so complex that it can't be stated simply, but as Somerset Maugham put it: "To write simply is as difficult as to be good." Though it is tempting to use professional jargon to sound more "authoritative," you will usually sound pompous and dull instead. Don't hide behind complex language.

Simplicity has power. One prominent Philadelphia lawyer made himself a fortune by putting this axiom into practice. At the turn of the century, people were suing railroad companies for deaths and injuries incurred at railroad crossings. The Pennsylvania Railroad Company hired the lawyer to write a legal notice that would tell pedestrians what their responsibilities were in averting accidents. His fee was $10,000.00, a lot of money, especially in those days, but a small price to pay for stemming the tide of liability suits. The company may have had second thoughts when they received the lawyer's notice. It was four words long: "Stop, Look, and Listen."

Yet these four words branded themselves on the mind of every American as no erudite dissertation could have done. Pedestrians became aware of their responsibilities. The accident rate at crossings fell. The tide of suits evaporated overnight. As the architect Mies van der Rohe said: "Less is more."

Eliminate unnecessary adjectives and adverbs. Nouns and verbs are more powerful without a lot of window-dressing. Compare:

The industrious maid gently but deliberately applied a hot iron to the trousers of her employer, Mr. King.	The maid pressed Mr. King's trousers.
Henry had the good fortune to discover a one-dollar bill lying on the sprawling thoroughfare.	Henry found a dollar on the street.

Eliminate unnecessary qualifiers. Be direct. Words like "almost," "nearly," "quite" and "somewhat" weaken your points and plant doubts in your listeners' minds. Compare:

She was quite overjoyed to receive the rather costly jewelry.	She loved receiving expensive jewelry.

Put your statements in positive form. A lot of negatives weaken your remarks. Compare:

He did not think that the film was interesting in the least.	He found the film uninteresting.

Use active constructions. They sound simpler, more direct, more energetic. Compare:

(PASSIVE)	(ACTIVE)
The ball is watched by the batter.	The batter watches the ball.
My elders will always be respected by me.	I shall always respect my elders.

Flow

To make your presentation interesting, you need variety of language.

Vary the length of your sentences.

> Hitler said that as things develop he's going to wring England's neck like a chicken. Some chicken. Some neck.
>
> —Winston Churchill

> Grenada, we were told, is a friendly island paradise for tourism. Well it wasn't. It was a Soviet-Cuban colony being readied as a major military bastion to export terror and undermine democracy.
>
> We got there just in time.
>
> —President Reagan,
> October 28, 1983

To check for monotony of length, look at your sentence structure on the page and listen to yourself speaking your remarks on tape.

Move from the abstract to the concrete, from the general to the specific. An example:

> These are perilous times. Inflation is wreaking havoc with the economy, diplomacy remains ineffective in the face of international skirmishes, babies are starving and the common man is afraid to walk the streets at night.

Explain the unfamiliar in familiar terms:

> What is a trillion? Now we all know that a billion is a thousand million and a trillion is a thousand billion, that's easy. But ... we couldn't

really envision a trillion [so] we did it in time. If somebody was born
when Jesus Christ was born and had lived all this time and started
counting seconds—"1 . . . 2 . . . 3 . . . 4" he'd be up to 62.5 billion right
now, which is 6¼ percent of a trillion. It takes 31,700 years to count
a trillion seconds. Now that's 317 centuries and we're in the 20th, so
it's the same old 6 percent. It keeps coming back to you.

—"The Problem of Big Government"
J. Peter Grace
Economic Club of Detroit
March 18, 1985

Focus

Keep your listener focused on what you are saying and where you are
going.

Make smooth transitions that lead him firmly from section to section.
This means from introduction to body, between sections of the body, and
from the body to the conclusion.

Your transitions should be like guideposts that remind the listener of
where you have been, and point to where you're going.

Coal may be our most immediately available alternative energy source,
but solar holds the way to our energy future.

But enough of the past. Let us take a look at the future.

Use a recurring phrase, question or set of images to give your speech
a through-line. A through-line is the continuous connection that gives
sensible progression to changing thoughts. In his Lincoln Memorial
address, Martin Luther King, Jr., kept a through-line going with his
repetition of the phrase "I have a dream."

Clarence Darrow, in a speech defending a young black man on trial
for murder, asked repeatedly, "What has Harry Sweet done?" and varied
that question linking Sweet's position to the larger issues of justice,
racism and moral responsibility.

What would you have done [in Henry Sweet's position]?

> The law has made [the Negro] equal, but man has not. And, after all,
> the last analysis is—what has man done?—not what has the law done?

Use repetition and rhyme to keep your listener's ear focused. Examples of each:

> We shall fight on the beaches, we shall fight on the landing grounds,
> we shall fight in the fields and streets, we shall fight in the hills, we
> shall never surrender...

> —Winston Churchill

> Ulster will fight, and Ulster will be right!

> —Lord Randolph Churchill

Highlights

Use the following attention-getting tactics to get and keep the audience involved throughout the course of your talk.

Tell a personal, moving story.

> In the early 1900's I was brought to this country by my parents to
> escape the tortuous "pogroms" waged against the Jews in Russia. My
> brother, I and the other immigrant youngsters were eager to share in
> the freedom of the land of opportunity—and there was opportunity!
> We would go to school, to the neighborhood houses, to libraries. We
> burned with the desire to learn.

> One day, when I was about eight or nine, I made my usual journey to
> the 10th Street Library, on the Lower East Side. But this time the
> librarian stopped me at the front door. She asked to see my hands.
> "They're not clean enough," she said. So I ran home, ran up our five
> flights of stairs, washed them and ran back to the library. Again the
> librarian asked to see my hands, and again she said they weren't clean
> enough! Again I ran home, up the stairs, washed them, down the stairs
> and back to the library. Again I was refused admittance. After the
> third try I quit. Years later it dawned on me that the librarian was
> sending kids home because the library was overcrowded with all the
> children who loved to go there.

Is the love of learning as strong today as it was then? Obviously it is in the young man I am here to honor...

—Irving J. Katz,
Humanities Award
Address,
Midwood High School
Brooklyn, New York, 1955

Create curiosity with a controversial statement:

The state of California spends more than $4 billion every year on MediCal... and [Dr. Edward Rubin has been] building an empire on these dollars... his medical financial practice has been under scrutiny for years. Nonetheless, he continues to operate...

—"60 Minutes," on
Edward Rubin, M.D.

Ask a controversial question:

Would you like the government to stop supporting college education [meaning that only certain people could attend institutions of higher learning]?

State a striking fact or statistic:

Do you know there are more rats than people in New York City?

—Robert Kennedy at a
business luncheon in
Vincennes, Indiana

Just remember that the statistics you use must be geared to your audience. A presentation filled with highly technical figures on the gold market might be a piece of cake for an audience of financiers, but utterly incomprehensible to the general public. You should also make sure that you use the same units (denominations) for both terms in any comparison. Don't, for instance, try to compare fractions and percentages, bushels and tons, yards and miles.

Refer to famous quotations, or even turn them around for effect:

I've never seen more of less.

> —An architect describing
> what he considered to be
> a particularly boring
> monument, in reference to
> Mies van der Rohe's
> proverbial "Less is more"

If we cannot now end our differences, at least we can help make the world safe for diversity.

> —President Kennedy's deliberate
> reversal of Woodrow Wilson's
> stated ambition to make the
> world "safe for democracy"

Sum up a point with a pithy epigram:

Nothing lasts like temporary.

> —Diplomatic saying

In finance, everything that is agreeable is unsound and everything that is sound is disagreeable.

> —Winston Churchill

Look for and use memorable labels:

Iron curtain

> —Winston Churchill

MBWA: Management by Walking Around

> —Peters and Waterman

Give a definition that does more than define, that appeals to the imagination. Walter Heller, chairman, Council of Economic Advisors, defined economic growth as "the pot of gold and the rainbow."

Use a striking metaphor, an analogy or an image that appeals to the senses:

The rest of mankind is the carving knife while we are the fish and the meat.

> —Sun Yat-sen to an audience
> of Chinese followers

It is easy enough to say that man is mortal simply because he will endure, that when the last ding-dong of doom has clanged and faded from the last worthless rock hanging tideless in the last red and dying evening, that even then there will be one more sound—that of his puny inexhaustible voice, still talking.

> —William Faulkner,
> Nobel Prize acceptance speech

Ask a series of questions:

What do you prefer: that we keep Social Security the way it is now? Or we change it to a totally different system? Would you rather pay a higher Social Security Tax now so that in forty or fifty years you'll be taken care of? Or would you like to know that the retirement age will be sixty-seven instead of sixty-five?

> —Senator Bill Bradley,
> Leadership Seminar
> for High School Seniors,
> Paterson, New Jersey

Humor

"I'll start with a joke and warm up the audience" is a phrase I hear often. Certainly, healthy laughter is a way of bringing people together. But unless there is an organic connection between your joke, your subject and you, it will be recognized for what it is, a contrivance.

You are not a stand-up comic, nor are you expected to be. Good comics agonize over the quality of their material. It is very difficult to be funny. So why should you expect satire, surprise, exaggeration and other elements of humor to come rolling off your tongue without a lot of hard work and research?

The definition of humor is not narrowly confined to just the telling of jokes. Humor includes irony, understatement, appreciation of life's foibles, the simple, "awful" truth and a clever use of self-deprecation.

I am reminded of the time the late Jessica Savitch took advantage of a moment to turn self-deprecation into humor. She was David Letterman's guest on his late-night show. In fine fettle, mixing good cheer with information, she described how she chose her wardrobe for the "NBC Nightly News." Then abruptly her mood changed, and she admitted she felt ill at ease. When Letterman asked her why, she pulled out a typed lineup for the show, which stated the order of guest appearances, time allotments, and so on. "I found this format," she said, and proceeded to read it out loud: "'First segment, interview with Jessica Savitch, second segment, interview with Jessica Savitch,' then down a little further it says, 'third segment, Jessica continued or Bob the dog.'" Turning to the audience, Jessica said, "So this means, folks, if I do well I'll be back for segment three, and you'll know if I don't do well because Bob the dog will be here instead." The audience burst into laughter and applause.

The annoyances we experience when we travel are made a bit more bearable when we realize others share our feelings. In an essay entitled "Chicago," Charles Kuralt, CBS Anchorman, describes the typical hotel room with thin walls. He can hear the fellow in the next room taking a shower, having a fight with his wife over the telephone, and so on. Kuralt begins to dream:

"In the perfect hotel room, the laundry bags would accommodate more than one shirt and one pair of socks before tearing. The maids would not congregate outside my door at 6:30 A.M. to laugh and chat, and they would not knock at 7:00 A.M. to see if the DO NOT DISTURB sign is on there by accident. There would not be a picture of Montmartre on the wall of the ideal hotel room, or, indeed, a picture of any other place in France. Once, in a string of Holiday Inns across four states in the Middle West, I got the same picture of Montmartre five nights in a row.

"In the hotel room of my dreams, I could turn down the heat, and— I hesitate even to mention it—I could actually open the window. Probably that's going too far.

"Well the guy in the next room has finished his shower. Now I can hear him putting on his socks."*

Smiles of recognition are more desirable than humor that is squeezed out. My advice is to look to yourself for humor. You may not lead an audience to uproarious laughter, but you can give them a glimpse of how you look at life and experience its foibles as well as its joys. That in itself is pleasurable. Leave the joke books to the writers of them. Granted, a wonderful, appropriate story that matches your intelligence and taste is delectable. I'm all for humor, but not the contrived kind.

You—with your perceptions, beliefs, values, and knowledge—are your most valuable resource as a speaker. Learning how to connect to yourself, the circumstances surrounding the occasion, and your audience is the first step to becoming real.

You owe it to your listeners to take that step. As Lew Sarett, one of my professors at Northwestern University, said: "If you give a speech that's 20 minutes long to an audience of 100 people, that's 2,000 minutes (33½ hours) of time you are taking out of the lives of your listeners—time that could be spent thinking, working, creating, experiencing. Time that is never going to come again. You'd better make it worthwhile!"

I would like to add this thought to Sarett's insight: even when you are speaking to a single colleague, you are using up time that could be spent in a dozen other valuable ways. *Design* your remarks and you'll prove yourself worth listening to. You'll prove yourself of value.

But your homework isn't done yet. Whether you read your speech from a text or deliver it extemporaneously, you will need to create a visual guide, something to give you confidence and keep you on track. Let's see how it's done.

*Charles Kuralt, *Dateline America* (Harcourt Brace Jovanovich, 1979), p. 122

Chapter Four

YOUR VISUAL GUIDE

(Step Two)

Behind making your own stuff there's another level: making your own tools to make your own stuff.

—Stewart Brand
The Last Whole Earth Catalogue

"**A**n oral agreement is not worth the paper it's written on!" said Sam Goldwyn of Metro-Goldwyn-Mayer in a classic malapropism. Well, I believe that oral *communication* is worth more, and is much more effective, when backed up by something written on paper.

Whenever you speak for professional purposes—giving a presentation at a meeting, or even speaking on the phone—it's a good idea to have a visual guide in front of you. It can be anything from a note with three key points jotted down to a full outline, from a memo to a completely written-out text. Something thought out and written down before you speak will be of great help to you.

Your visual guide becomes a road map that reminds you where you want to go and how to get there. It keeps you from getting lost or sidetracked along the way. With a good visual guide you don't have to struggle to remember the key phrases you want to use, because the phrases are there and your meaning stands out. Within the structure of your guide, you have the freedom to be real and to think your remarks through as you give them. You'll be clearer, more in touch with your audience and more alive.

OUTLINES

It is almost always preferable to use an outline rather than a written-out word-for-word text. The exceptions are scientific papers, financial statements or complicated material that has the listener weighing your every word. But for most occasions, a well-constructed, well-conceived outline is a better tool. Your eye sweeps down the page, and you can see where you're supposed to go. You can direct the flow of your thoughts. You can pay more attention to your listeners because you don't have your nose stuck to the page, and because you are not bound by a completely fixed text, *you are forced to think*, rather than read perfunctorily. In other words, you can speak *extemporaneously*. (Most people use the word "extemporaneous" to mean spontaneous or impromptu speaking; however, like other speech specialists, I use the term to mean *prepared* speaking and I use it quite broadly to include not only formal speeches but any speaking occasion in business or elsewhere in which you want to present a body of information.)

Include whatever facts and phrases you personally need in your outline, such as key thoughts and transitional sentences that will help you achieve a smooth, clean delivery. You shouldn't have to struggle to remember anything while speaking. A number of my clients write out all their transitional sentences since these tend to slip the mind; for others this might be unnecessary. Remember: These notes are for you. Let your needs and habits be your only criteria in formulating your visual guide.

At an informal meeting, discussion or interview you may find that 3×5 or 5×8 note cards are more convenient than an awkward sheaf of papers. You can also use note cards to refresh your memory before and

For Rob
Who taught me to believe that
anything is possible